HIGHER DENSITY HOUSING
PLANNING · DESIGN · MARKETING

National Association of Home Builders
15th and M Streets, N.W.
Washington, D.C. 20005

Higher Density Housing: Planning, Design, Marketing
ISBN 0-86718-271-7
Library of Congress Catalog Card Number 86-063356

Copyright © 1986 by the
National Association of Home Builders
of the United States
15th and M Streets, N.W.
Washington, D.C. 20005

When ordering this publication, please provide the
following information:

Title
ISBN 0-86718-271-7
Price
Quantity
NAHB membership number (as it appears on the
    Builder or *Nation's Building News* label)
Mailing address (including street number and zip
code)

Cover: See Figure 41

Higher Density Housing

Planning, Design, Marketing

Contents

Figures

Planning

Design

Marketing

Acknowledgments

Higher Density Housing: Planning, Design, Marketing represents a team effort by NAHB staff past and present. It had long been the goal of the NAHB publishing services, land use and environmental affairs, and technical services departments to publish a comprehensive guide to higher density housing. This book is the realization of our goal.

Special thanks are due to Sanford R. Goodkin, chairman of The Goodkin Group (La Jolla, CA), who contributed his expertise as author of the market research chapter and the marketing section. He was assisted by Mark Rodman Smith, vice president of The Goodkin Group. The Goodkin Group acknowledges the MIRM (Member, Institute of Residential Marketing) certificate program of southern California as a source of materials and ideas.

Michael Shibley, director of land use and environmental affairs for NAHB, provided invaluable assistance in writing the text and selecting illustrations. NAHB publications director Susan Bradford wrote portions of the text and edited the manuscript. Former NAHB staff members who contributed to the book while still at NAHB include Steve Moore (former NAHB program manager for architectural design, now with Hansen & Horn in Indianapolis) and Jim Van Zee (former NAHB land use planning specialist, now with the Urban Land Institute in Washington, D.C.)

Numerous architecture, planning, and building firms contributed illustrations to this book. Their work is credited as it appears throughout the text.

Higher Density Housing: Planning, Design, Marketing was prepared under the general direction of Kent W. Colton, NAHB executive vice president, by the following staff members:

William D. Ellingsworth, senior staff vice president, Public Affairs
Denise L. Darling, staff vice president, Publishing Services
Susan D. Bradford, director, Publications
Michael F. Shibley, director, Land Use and Environmental Affairs
David Rhodes, director, Art

Introduction

Well-designed and quality-built higher density housing is an asset to consumers and communities alike. In an era of rising land and construction costs and shifting demographics, higher density development fills an important niche in the housing marketplace.

Higher density development appeals to today's consumers for a number of reasons. It offers the traditional lifestyle benefits of homeownership, such as privacy and security, without the maintenance requirements of a conventional large-lot single-family home. Higher density housing also tends to be more affordable than conventional subdivision homes, and provides buyers with the convenience and stability of neighborhoods. Most importantly, higher density housing brings a piece of the American Dream to a large cross-section of the homebuying public: the pride of owning their own home.

Higher density housing is an effective way to meet the shelter needs of the community as well. It allows the distribution of development costs over a greater number of units, and concentrates growth in areas that are well served by available public services. Higher density development can also support a number of amenities, such as commercial centers and recreational facilities, that are not usually found in conventional single-family developments.

"Higher Density" Defined

This publication considers both detached and attached housing within the context of "higher density." Single-family detached homes at densities of 7-12 units per acre, such as zero lot line and patio homes, are discussed. Attached housing, including duplexes, triplexes, quadruplexes, townhouses, and stacked flats, are also considered, at densities ranging from 5-30 units per acre.

The concept of "higher density" has different applications in different communities. For example, if a local zoning ordinance stipulates that the minimum lot size within a given zone is 10,000 square feet, the resulting density is approximately 4 units per acre. In this instance, a density of 6-8 units per acre would be considered higher density. In another community, higher density might mean something much greater, such as 18 units per acre.

The point to remember is that density is a relative term and should be considered within the parameters of the individual community. Attempting to change or increase densities within existing communities will almost always meet with local opposition. When presenting higher density to the public, builder/developers must clearly define their terms. They should be careful not to give the impression that they want to change the entire housing image of the community, when in fact, they may be seeking only minor increases in density.

This book will attempt to present a range of higher density options that can be applied within any locality. While the principles of higher density are universal, they must be tailored to the needs of the individual community.

Scope of the Book

Much has been written about the theory of higher density development: its history, how and why it "should" work. This book tells builder/developers how to *make* higher density housing work in virtually any community. Using a practical, nuts-and-bolts approach, it presents detailed information on planning, designing, and marketing higher density homes. Needless to say, financing is a critical element in the success of any development project as well. As a planning, design, and marketing guide, however, this book does not attempt to address financing techniques. NAHB's publication *Financing Land Acquisition and Development* provides this information with a detailed discussion of the various financing options available to builder/developers.

Higher Density Housing is divided into three parts:

Planning In this section, traditional community objections to higher density housing are examined, with recommendations on how to overcome them. This section also contains a thorough discussion of market research: why it is a fundamental step in the higher density development process, how to conduct it, and how to use the results to maximum advantage. The approval process is also reviewed, with a discussion of problems builder/developers commonly face and how to solve them.

Design This section discusses the design program: establishing project theme and putting the design team together. The various higher density housing types, both detached and attached, are examined in depth. Exterior and interior design considerations are addressed, as are public service provisions for higher density communities.

Marketing This section covers marketing, the final step in higher density development. The marketing plan and its implementation are examined in detail, with special attention given to budgets and controls, traffic and sales goals, pricing, merchandising and presentation, advertising, promotion, sales, public relations, and post-sale relations.

Higher Density Housing: Planning, Design, Marketing concludes with a glossary of terms commonly used in the development of higher density housing, and a selected bibliography of additional readings.

Audience

Higher Density Housing: Planning, Design, Marketing was written primarily for the small- to medium-volume builder/developer who is familiar with conventional single-family housing and wants to move into higher density development.

The book will also be useful for public officials, regulators, and consumers as a thorough introduction to the advantages of higher density housing.

SUBDIVISION FEATURES

Maintenance Fee:	$25.00 / QUARTER *	
Pool	Sauna	Spa
Rec. Room	Tennis	Putting Green
Security		

*FEE COVERS ROOF INS.& STREET UPKEEP

Driveway	ASPHALT
Parking	3 CAR GARAGE
Fencing Height	NONE
Landscaping	NONE
Balcony:	NO Patio: NO
Roof Type:	
Utility Room Location	IN HOUSE
Washer/Dryer	NONE
Walk-in Closet:	MASTER OTHER
Flooring	CRPTS/TILE ENT. & KIT.
Luminous Lighting:	KITCHEN BATH
Heating:	F/A Air Cond. INCLUDED
Tub Type and Surrounding	PORC/CERAMIC TILE
Shower	TILE
Pullman Tops	CERAMIC TILE
Counter Tops	CERAMIC TILE
Pantry	CUPBOARD
Sinks	DBL/PORCELAIN
Oven Brand of Type	G.E./SGL/ELC/S.C.
Microwave:	OPTIONAL
Dishwasher Brand or Cycle	G.E./2 CYCLE
Fireplace	WOODBURNING

Planning

1. Community Attitudes

From its beginnings in New York City, zoning has been viewed as a discriminatory tool used to exclude "undesirable elements" from certain areas of the community. Over the years, zoning provisions in many communities have effectively denied lower-income and minority households the opportunity for decent, affordable homes.

More recently, tradition-bound zoning policies have affected middle-class households as well, owing to the high interest rates of the late 1970s and early 1980s. First-time buyers were not able to qualify for the purchase of the house they wanted: a big house on a big lot.

Increasingly, however, states are recognizing the restrictive nature of zoning regulations. Through court and legislative remedies, local governments are being forced to expand the range of housing choices available to all persons, regardless of ethnicity or income level. It is clear that local governments must do their part by planning for higher density housing that is both cost-effective and responsive to a variety of housing needs.

Traditional Community Objections

Despite the documented benefits of higher density development, many communities resist residential growth of any type. New development represents a departure from tradition, and longtime residents fear a disruption of their accustomed lifestyle. Even relative newcomers express concern that growth will change the character of the community in which they have chosen to live.

In some cases, resistance to new development is based on prejudice, presumed differences in income level, or the belief that the new homes will be of lower quality than the existing housing stock. These attitudes are generally due to a lack of understanding of higher density housing and the level of quality it represents. Those who view higher density housing to be substandard fear that it will eventually lead to a rise in crime and a decline in property values. Interestingly, however, many of the nation's older, stable inner-city neighborhoods and close-in suburbs are themselves "higher density," consisting of 5,000 square-foot or smaller lots (Figure 1).

Finally, new development—especially higher density—is perceived as a fiscal and physical drain on the community. Yet opponents of higher density development often do not recognize that the standards that guided the growth of the nation's older single-family neighborhoods were nonscientific and reflected what was affordable, marketable, and developable during the 1950s, 60s and 70s (Figure 2). In an era of relatively inexpensive land, energy, and financing, it was logical and desirable from both the

Figure 1. Older, higher density urban neighborhood offers safe, stable living environment

Figure 2. Underregulated suburban sprawl

builder's and consumer's perspective to provide the maximum lot per dollar invested. Not surprisingly, the regulatory framework supported large-lot, sprawl development.

Benefits to the Community

Most zoning regulations today continue to reflect the standards of a generation ago. They establish residential densities at a predetermined number of dwelling units per acre and fail to recognize the difference between dwelling units and the number of people per unit. Since higher density dwellings are usually smaller than conventional units, they generally appeal to small families and mean fewer school children per unit and lower traffic generation per unit.

Unfortunately, citizen groups and local officials often do not acknowledge the demographic characteristics of higher density development during rezoning or subdivision hearings. Instead of focusing on the intensity of development and the actual demand a particular project generates, decision makers focus their attention on the density itself.

Many communities consider density and intensity to be the same. *The intensity* of development refers to the level of use of the land, a broader concept than *density,* which is simply units per acre. Industrial and commercial uses, for example, are considered in terms of intensity. Floor area ratios can be used to define the relationship between the level of development and the site. Some members of the development industry have suggested that this approach be substituted for conventional density calculations in residential development, since the density numbers frequently misrepresent the actual intensity of proposed use.

Public Services

Under a higher density development scheme, the demand for public services—particularly recreational and transportation facilities—is often reduced. Higher density developments, whether a large planned community or an individual cluster, frequently offer private recreational facilities. Paid for by project residents, these facilities can range from multipurpose courts and swimming pools to large parks for passive and active recreation (Figure 3). The economy-of-scale benefits of higher density development cannot generally be matched in the conventional single-family subdivision.

The benefits of concentration also hold for highways and roads. In a higher density project the same length of road can serve more residences. While individual intersections or road segments must sometimes accommodate greater traffic volume in a higher density development, it is more cost-effective for a highway department to redesign an intersection or provide a traffic light than to widen several miles of highway.

In some cases, developers are forced by local regulations to provide private streets to serve the higher density units they are building. These private streets are paid for and maintained by the residents, further reducing the demand for local services but placing a greater financial burden upon the buyer. Since private streets are often required to be built to

public standards, however, they should be accepted for public maintenance.

Buyers in some higher density communities prefer private streets for the air of exclusivity and individuality they convey. Local government regulations often prohibit private streets, however, because officials fear that residents will petition at some later point for public street status. Yet officials are reluctant to modify their standards to permit such streets as a matter of right. Public services are discussed in greater detail in the Design section.

Setback Requirements

Many of the yard setback and lot requirements set forth in zoning regulations are as outmoded as the density standards that continue to guide today's development. Setback and frontage requirements, for example, were originally intended to allow for the widening of roads as traffic demand warranted. They also reflected a concern for light, air, space, and

sanitation. New technology and new design techniques have eliminated the need for conventional setback requirements.

Contemporary transportation design provides for a hierarchy of highways that eliminates residences from arterial or major collector roads. Setbacks from residential streets have thus become a function of the need for off-street parking. Recent studies have shown that the excessive setback requirements found in many local regulations add a significant cost factor to the price of a finished house. For example, utility line installation is affected by setback requirements, as are paving areas for driveways and sidewalks. The greater the setback, the more expensive the construction costs to provide these items.

The trend toward smaller lots and smaller houses at higher densities addresses the setback issue by providing for more compact development. The buyer benefits from cost savings in the purchase price; local government, from reduced maintenance costs.

2. Market Research

This chapter briefly discusses elements of residential market research and analysis. It provides a framework builder/developers can use to analyze their markets and reduce the risks that are inherent in real estate development. The chapter also gives insights into the research process so that builder/developers can better utilize the services of a market research company.

Before launching any multi-million dollar project, it is wise to examine the market for which the product is intended. Opportunities to increase market capture can be maximized when a project is designed specifically for its given marketplace, and properly marketed and merchandised to respective market segments.

So it is with higher density housing. By conducting market research before a development plan is formulated, a builder/developer can better design a project to respond to market opportunities. Higher density housing can be extremely successful if certain psychological and economic characteristics are taken into consideration. For example, there are two major markets for higher density: first-time buyers, who require entry-level pricing, and the contracting family (usually empty-nesters, pre-retirees, divorcees, retirees) who want high quality features in a smaller living space.

While many people still prefer large-lot detached housing because of the perception of privacy and greater prestige, it is important to remember that the marketplace is not homogeneous. Rather, it consists of a variety of consuming groups who require a variety of housing types, including higher density. Market research is the science—and art—of bringing together product and market.

Who Should Conduct Market Research

Depending on a company's size, market research can be handled in-house or by an outside consultant. A small company may not have the capital to hire market research professionals. Many builder/developers find, however, that comprehensive market research requires staff time and expertise beyond their in-house capabilities. The argument can be made that market research conducted by an outside consultant pays for itself in increased sales. It also

provides an independent third-party analysis for use by lenders or joint venture partners, architects and land planners.

Selecting a Market Researcher

The best way to find a market research consultant is by referral. The local home builders association or other professional associations may be able to provide names; fellow builders may also have suggestions. The yellow pages are a last resort. Once a market research firm has been identified:

- Ask for references—and check them.
- Meet with the person(s) who will be working on your project, and make sure that they understand your needs.
- Get all agreements in writing: specify due dates, prices, and type of research to be conducted.
- And finally, stay in frequent contact with the researcher(s) throughout the research and analysis phases to ensure that work is progressing according to the original agreement. Interaction between the builder/developer and the research organization enhances the service provided, yielding more valuable information.

How to Use Market Research

As the builder/developer works with the researcher to plan a market research strategy, certain basic elements must be considered.

Who will be the primary user of the information? For example, a lender is looking for precedents in the marketplace and statistical evidence that his/her risks have been carefully measured. A builder, on the other hand, strives for market entry and rapid absorption, so bottom line projections are vital.

The builder/developer's project team—architects, engineers, landscape architects, interior designers, and other professionals—can benefit from market research. A creative "team" approach to product development, starting with the market research phase, is helpful and welcomed by many of these professionals.

What should the research accomplish? What specific questions should it answer?

What is the condition of the marketplace in terms of:

- Products on the market (Figure 4)
    - Single-family detached
    - Single-family attached
    - Rental properties
- The resale market
    - How long homes are on the market before they are sold
    - Characteristics of resale homes
    - Asking and selling price
    - Most active areas, product type, and price range
- The competition—perform an audit of all competition, as discussed later in this chapter; see also Figure 10 to determine:
    - Their merchandising and marketing formats
    - Their locational advantages and disadvantages
    - Pricing, absorption, product mix
    - Financing plans they offer
    - Where their buyers are moving from (location and length of time they lived there)
    - Where their buyers work
    - Their buyer lifestyle, including types of recreation preferred, extent and formality of home entertainment, amount of traveling
    - Features buyers like and dislike about competitor communities
- Economic forces affecting market conditions (Figure 5)
    - Employment conditions
    - Job growth and employment centers
    - Characteristics of growth
    - Expansion of existing companies and arrival of new companies
    - Prevalence of two-income families
- Demographics (characteristics of the local population)
    - Total population
    - Population growth
    - Number of households
    - Household growth
    - Size of households
    - Household value
    - Average and median ages, and distribution of age by range
    - Average and median incomes, and distribution by range
    - Commute patterns
    - Length of residence
    - Distribution of housing types, including single-family, multifamily, and mobile homes

Combined, the above statistics can be used to analyze a market to determine who lives there now. These factors, combined with projected community trends, help determine who buyers will be in the marketplace.

Has the market been changing in any way? Are there new market segments? Identify specific market segments within the community. Figure 6 defines a

METROPOLITAN AREA 1976-1986 Year	Single-Family	Two-Family	Percent Single Family	Multi-Family	Percent Multi-Family	TOTAL UNITS
1976	14,966	716	54	13,504	46	29,186
1977	8,102	256	72	3,287	28	11,645
1978	8,536	214	93	675	7	9,420
1979	12,024	234	84	2,319	16	14,577
1980	20,052	306	86	3,207	14	23,565
1981	20,388	414	74	7,363	26	28,165
1982	16,488	450	76	5,265	24	22,203
1983	11,117	212	71	4,660	29	18,991
1984	11,573	156	77	3,552	23	15,281
1985	12,920	296	67	6,507	33	19,703
1986	23,664	532	75	8,211	25	32,237

Figure 4. Total New Residential Units

The Goodkin Group

LABOR MARKET AREA: 1985 - 1990 Occupation	1985	Projected 1990	% Change 1985-1990
Managers & Officers	74,206	87,688	18.2
Professional Occupations	143,150	166,924	16.6
Technical Occupations	32,968	38,551	16.9
Service Occupations	127,431	149,466	17.3
Maintenance & Production Occupations	227,133	267,846	17.9
Clerical Occupations	174,456	205,936	18.0
Sales Occupations	59,208	70,150	18.5
TOTAL*	838,552	986,561	17.7
Industry			
Mining	27,100	35,200	29.9
Construction	46,900	55,200	17.7
Manufacturing	127,400	148,000	16.2
Transporation, Communication Public Utilities	53,600	63,800	19.0
Trade	210,500	249,800	18.7
Finance, Insurance & Real Estate	61,300	73,700	20.2
Services	272,600	313,500	15.0
Government	72,800	82,600	13.5
TOTAL	872,200	1,021,800	17.2

*Occupational listings not additive to total.

Figure 5. Employment Projections by Occupation and Industry

The Goodkin Group

number of distinct homebuying segments that can be used when conducting market research.

Are there market opportunities that the competition has not discovered?

Can your company have a locational, price, or design advantage?

Will your company be introducing higher density housing to the community?

- If so, take full advantage of the opportunity to bring something new into the community.
- If not, how successful has higher density housing been thus far?

- How well have higher density homes done in the resale market? Determine whether they sold because of attractive pricing and financing, or if there is lasting marketability for higher density in the community.
- Have design and planning been a drawback to acceptance of higher density housing? If what has already been built in the community looks like traditional apartments and has no additional privacy, storage, or space, few people will want to move there.
- Are any luxury higher density products currently on the market? How have they sold?

Figure 6. Homebuying Segments

Segment/Household Size	Characteristics/Design Implications
Young Singles/1-2	Under 30; gregarious. Unmarried, active, mobile, many interests, entertain informally. Career experimentation and enhancement; loyal to career, not employer. Few possessions; spend generously on clothes and personal growth. *Design implications:* Glitz, color, excitement, variety, experimentation, interior privacy for sleep and bath. Frequent visitors; enjoy physical activity and leisure time. Emphasize living room area and master bedroom suite.
Adult Singles/1-2	Over 30, presently unmarried (single, widowed, separated, divorced). Serious social relationships, require privacy. More mature but still experimenting; early possession buildup. Appreciate quality and dependable brands. Read consumer reports and specialized magazines about their careers and leisure interests. Active with peer groups in sports and leisure. *Design implications:* Glitz, design animation in ceiling, floor, room shapes. Serious courting for serious reasons, so need interior privacy. Minimal daily maintenance, because workplace is center of peer group time and effort. Appreciate good designs in features like fireplace, bathrooms, built-ins, workspaces. Don't waste yards or hallways on them.
Young Marrieds Without Children/2	Mature discretionary/dual income. Physically active; entertain often, both formally and informally; independent, do-it-yourselfers, maybe a sports car. Planning for future: financial, career goals, family planning. Solid friendships at work. Ambitious, travel often. *Design implications:* The look of success; emphasize entry, indoor/outdoor relationships. Feature good wardrobe and storage space, combined living/dining room, master bedroom suite, den or family room, lots of usable space that is dramatic with plenty of decorating potential.
Young Marrieds With Child/3	Under 35, child under 5, both spouses working, entertain informally, amateur gardeners, focus on child, planning on more children. *Design implications:* Emphasize kitchen (good lighting, pleasant), informal dining area, master bedroom, similar secondary bedrooms, family room with fireplace, large yard. May have pet(s); need roaming space for pets and children. Provide interior mess (play) area.
Compact Family/3	Couple, age 35+, with one child. Adults outnumber children, so design house around adult activities. *Design implications:* Emphasize adult-oriented areas, informal dining with formal living, separation of master bedroom and secondary bedrooms. Large secondary bedroom preferred.
Move-Up Family/3-4	The "monthly payment" group. Nonemployed "housewife," focus on casual and informal family activities, numerous interests, mostly child-oriented. Amateur gardeners; transitional. *Design implications:* Emphasize kitchen, informal dining area, master bedroom, smaller secondary bedrooms, fireplace in family room, large yard.
Established Family/3-5+	Making monthly payments comfortably, some discretionary income, approaching their economic and social peak, some formal entertaining, older children/teenagers, many interests, 3-car family, prefer limited maintenance. *Design implications:* Separate formal living and dining areas, den or formal family room, separate master bedroom suite, large secondary bedrooms, formal yard.

Segment/Household Size	Characteristics/Design Implications
Luxury Family/2-4+	Have arrived, tremendous discretionary income, very formal house, don't entertain often but when they do, it's formal; teenagers (maybe a small child too), less physically active, one or two formal sports affiliations, dine out often, minimal maintenance, privacy mandatory. Can come in and out of market as they please; pampered, will not compromise on space, quality, or prestige of address. *Design implications:* Formal entry, separate living and dining rooms, den, master bedroom (possibly separate) plus retreat, guest or maid's room, privacy and security are important. Large walk-in wardrobes, gourmet kitchen, wine area, classic wetbar, formal entertainment room, library, paneling, fine woods in kitchen and bath cabinets and staircase. On exterior, strong window and roof treatments, wide facade impact. In condos, still luxurious rooms, but with less yard to maintain.
Move-Down Family/2-3	40-50 years old, leaving large family house, prefer limited maintenance, informal living and formal entertainment areas. Travel often, occasional visits from family or guests, focused active and passive recreation. *Design implications:* Quality not quantity, luxury. Focus on living room and master bedroom area, adequately large secondary areas, den, dining room and breakfast nook or informal eating area, small private patio. Have accumulated possessions and don't want to give them up, so storage is important. Separate his/her closets. Fireplace, bar, reading nook, skylights, nearby recreation, status neighborhood instead of space.
Divorcee/1+	Reestablishing social lifestyle, experimenting; may be looking for serious relationships. Want freedom to travel or pursue leisure interests; may be career-oriented with social life focused on workplace. *Design implications:* Home may be a "launching pad" for social experimentation; want smaller but full kitchen; master suite desirable for romance; need potential for rootedness and security from traditional room configurations. Provide closets (not necessarily large); a sense of pampering; larger tub with jacuzzi potential; use low-maintenance materials.
Single Female With Child/2+	Child-oriented. Must find a suitable place to live with child; child is focus of lifestyle; limited social life. *Design implications:* Privacy from child yet ability to monitor (no matter what age). Interior play area, important TV space. Bright, informal, easily maintained eating area with kitchen, no dining room, but perhaps an area for infrequent formal meals. Doesn't expect luxury, but appreciates appointments and materials above price range. Make-up area, separate storage and clothes closets for child and her, smaller secondary bedroom, prefers separate full bath for child.
Empty Nester-Never Nested/2	Mature, self-sufficient couple, no debts, occasional overnight guests, active in leisure activities, entertain often; want privacy, minimal maintenance and investment in house costs. Mobile in attitude but permanent in residence. *Design implications:* Formal living and dining areas, den, guest suite, large master suite and retreat, informal eating nook in kitchen, low-maintenance yard.
Young Retiree (Active)/2	Active in community, enjoy passive recreation, semiformal entertaining at home, privacy important, don't travel much. Often retired civil service or military in 40s and 50s, work part-time but enjoy some

Continued

Segment/Household Size	Characteristics/Design Implications
Young Retiree (Active)/2 Continued	sports (tennis, golf, swimming), people-oriented. *Design implications:* Quality rather than quantity, secondary bedrooms usable for hobbies too, option of separate master bedrooms (good-sized), storage space. Room configuration should be functional yet formal and traditional. Separate his/her closets, ordinary baths with limited sex appeal. One-car garage.
Passive Retiree/2	Not physically able to engage in active sports. Prefer walking, family and group activities, cardplaying, reading, travel. *Design implications:* Avoid stairs and heights. Conservative one-story and end units are preferred. Grab bars and other safety features should be subtle in design. Interior privacy is important; also, separate (and equal) bedrooms. Include a garden or patio area and a nicely lighted, full but compact kitchen (not too small). Good window treatment is appreciated. Lower appliance shelves, pantries and switches.
Widow-Widower/1	Initial period of severe readjustment followed by "life goes on;" reexamination of friendships and purpose of life. Budget-conscious and will listen to advice; privacy and comfort are important. *Design implications:* Interior privacy; no fanciness unless affluent. Wants a full kitchen and has time for maintenance. Wants a feeling of home, a fireplace; tends to use formal areas rarely, so living and dining rooms can be smaller; has possessions that are vital links to past, so needs wall space and storage. Security features appreciated; perhaps a hobby or work area; extra sleeping area for visiting children or guests. Neighborhood very important.

Special Homebuying Segments*

Second Homebuyers-National Origin/2 +	Affluent empty nesters who travel, pre-retirees, active retirees, self-employed, corporate chiefs. *Design implications:* Spacious luxury, detached home, many amenities, with view of golf course or other premium features.
Second Homebuyers-Regional Origin/2 +	Often same as above, but in lower income bracket. *Design implications:* Compact luxury, usually attached units, turnkey delivery as an option (with furnishings).
Investors	Local and out-of-state. Many may eventually live in community where investment home is located.
Aesthetics/1-2 +	Often single, with a profession as a writer, artist, musician, architect, decorator, or similar. Borderline or actual elitist. Freedom and the avant-garde are important to them. *Design implications:* Thematic architecture or traditional with strong architectural feeling: wood, masonry, roof lines, animation, fireplace, interior garden, circular staircase, lofts, beams, clerestory, skylight, or other natural design elements. Provide a work area. Choose thematic decoration, such as Oriental. Likes to be in peer group neighborhood.

* These are important, identifiable segments in many regional marketplaces. Since they can represent a large part of a higher density project's target market, their needs should be carefully addressed.

Segment/Household Size	Characteristics/Design Implications
Glitz/1-2+	Seek that which is new and "in." Gregarious. Spend much of their income. *Design implications:* Heavy design and merchandising orientation. Sell show-off features with "sizzle:" mirrors, chrome, avant-garde, entertainment, balcony or interior decks to view guests, music room, large TV, bar, European kitchen with every gimmick, wine rack.
Boomers/1-4+	78 million post-WWII baby boomers, ages 20-39. Beware of stratifying them beyond the segments below, because they are found in many different market groups (except retirees. But in the year 2012, their median age will be 55—then watch the boom in the retirement, travel, tourism, recreation, and resort markets). 70 percent of the women are in the work force. Individual incomes are unimpressive, but when combined through marriage, 30 percent have a household income of $30,000 or more. 51 percent live in someone else's household (often a parent), only 8 percent live alone and only 18 percent head their own households. 59 percent of female boomers are married and 76 percent of these have one or more children. Approximately 6 percent of boomers are young affluent urban professionals.
Young Boomers/1-3+	Aged 20-29, focus on workplace and career development, gaining maturity but still experimenting, somewhat egocentric. 45 percent of these households have children. Median household income is $17,800; will follow tradition to become homeowners as soon as they can afford to. *Design implications:* Singles will postpone home purchase for immediate gratification of clothes, travel, recreation, spouse-searching. This is an excellent apartment market: offer touches of luxury so they can feel that their jobs pay off. Otherwise similar to other young segments.
Older Boomers/3-5+	Aged 30-39 and much more settled, assured of their careers and their personal lives. 68 percent of these households have children under 18. Median household income is $24,800 and can expand rapidly. Similar to other young married segments.
Snowbirds and Desert Rats	Fall into two groups: fun-loving escapists and self-gratifying achievers. Fun-lovers of all ages have a vacation mentality, want to live out their fantasies, travel to experience different locations and ways of life. *Design implications:* both unusual and traditional interior and exterior designs. Feature drama: partying rooms, bold masonry fireplaces (with woodbox), lofts that convert to sleeping areas, lots of natural wood. Small spaces are fine as long as they're fun. Location is all-important; try timeshare. Self-gratifiers of all ages want to live their fantasies now, transfer work ethic into wish fulfillment. Often singles and divorcees, ambitious, heavy investors in brand-name material goods for prestige and comfort. *Design implications:* Showcase entertainment areas, bar, gourmet kitchen with European styling, worksaving appliances. Feature fireplaces, wood beams and paneling, good ceiling height, lots of closet space. Want to be seen and appreciated for their accomplishments. They spend beyond their means, so will accept rental unit that satisfies their lifestyle and location needs.

The Goodkin Group

Figure 7. Population and Household Demand

U.S. Census
Urban Decision Systems, Inc.
The Goodkin Group

YEAR:	1970	1980	1984 (est.)	1989 (proj.)
Population	125,961	151,323	160,893	172,745
Growth 1984-1989	11,852 people			
Annual Growth 1984-1989	2,370 people			
Households	35,206	50,967	54,834	59,705
Growth 1984-1989	4,871 units			
Annual Growth 1984-1989	974 units			

Figure 8. Projected Employment by Economic Sector

The Goodkin Group

1970-2000   (Number in Thousands)

Employment Sector	1970	1980	1990	2000
Mining	4.90	18.12	27.90	33.60
Contract Construction	28.00	46.20	71.40	85.40
Manufacturing	85.90	104.30	181.30	234.40
Transporation and Public Utilites	76.40	65.40	71.80	92.40
Wholesale and Retail Trade	118.00	181.50	272.40	357.50
Finance, Insurance and Real Estate	29.80	53.90	80.20	104.00
Services	88.40	167.80	229.10	312.90
Government	90.50	137.50	172.20	223.20
Total Non-Ag Wage And Salary	481.50	794.78	1116.30	1412.40
Agriculture (3)	6.50	5.80	5.10	4.00
Military (3)	10.10	11.10	11.10	11.10
All Other (3) (4)	40.70	57.50	76.10	97.00
TOTAL EMPLOYED (NUMBER OF JOBS)	1060.70	1643.90	2314.90	2967.90

Useful Sources of Market Data

The market researcher can draw on numerous free or low-cost sources to answer the economic and demographic questions discussed above. These sources include:

U.S. Census
Local chamber of commerce
State and local economic development agencies
Local utilities
Title companies
Local universities (unpublished studies as well as
    published reports)
Moving companies
Furniture stores
Board of education
Telephone company
State or U.S. Department of Labor or
    Employment Services
Local news clippings and real estate sections
Local legal newspapers and transcripts
Local bank reports

The researcher then analyzes the data gathered from these sources, possibly with the aid of a computer. The computer digests the information, cross-references it, and produces reports that provide valuable trends and indications for the builder/developer (see Figures 7-9).

Figure 9. Projected Housing Unit Demand

		Actual			Projected	
COUNTY STATISTICS 1970-2000	1970	1980	1983		1990	2000
Total Population	8.40	25.20	31.50		104.70	196.50
LESS: Non-Household Population	0.06	0.10	0.10		0.11	0.13
Household Population	8.30	25.10	31.40		104.60	196.40
Average Household Size	3.30	3.19	3.07		3.00	3.00
Households (Occupied Units)	2527.30	7868.30	10228.00		34863.30	65456.70
Vacancy Factor	5.00	5.00	5.00		5.00	5.00
Total Housing Units	2653.60	8261.80	10739.40		36604.50	68729.50
Incremental Demand Per Period	-	5608.10	2477.70		25867.10	3213.00
ANNUAL DEMAND	-	560.80	825.90		3695.30	3212.30
ANNUAL SINGLE FAMILY DEMAND	-	454.30	669.00		2993.20	2602.00
ANNUAL MULTI-FAMILY DEMAND	-	106.60	156.90		702.10	610.30

The Goodkin Group

Other Elements of Market Research

In addition to the market research strategies already discussed, the builder/developer should consider other elements to ensure a comprehensive market profile. These include consumer research, competitive audit, and absorption projections.

Consumer Research

Many builders don't even bother with consumer research. Yet no other manufacturer will engage in product output before knowing the profile of his/her prospective buyers. The best way to do this is, simply, to talk to the people who are interested in your product.

The builder/developer must establish an objective for developing consumer information, because the objective frequently determines the research techniques to be used. Two major approaches to research include shopper surveys and consumer surveys.

Shopper surveys can take place at your existing project, a competing project, or at other high traffic areas such as shopping malls. They ask about prospect preferences and reactions to your product. If certain patterns emerge, these can be accommo-

dated in your community. Consumer surveys can be performed at competitive communities. Findings are then incorporated into the overall project scheme.

Focus group interviews are an in-depth, qualitative research method conducted by well trained group leaders. Select 10-15 random names from your prospect list, and invite them to an informal evening session to learn more about your product. Show them attractive renderings of the homes as well as specific site plans and floor plans. A skilled group leader will be able to develop a profile of the target consumer's homebuying needs, preferences, and motivations based on several of these focus group interviews. The results will be intuitive rather than statistical—an invaluable addition to other market research findings.

Below are some of the techniques often used in consumer research:

● Traffic analysis of prospects circulating in the marketplace. What drew them to your product? How far were they willing to travel to see the product? What did they like and dislike about it?

Traffic analysis should take place over a four-weekend period at points of sale, with followup once a month for the subsequent four months. Traffic analysis can also be used to test the effectiveness of advertising, merchandising, and salesmanship.

- Move-in analysis of buyers at competitive projects with similar characteristics to yours. Why did they choose the competition rather than your product? Where did they live before? How far are they willing to commute to their workplace? Within which market segments do they fall?
- Mail and telephone interviews using mailing lists developed with professional help. Mailing lists are available for almost any socioeconomic category of prospects.

For the consumer research phase of the market analysis, budget $5.00 to $30.00 per interview, including computer time. Interpretation must be the work of skilled analysts rather than "number crunching" statisticians. Consumer research should take between three and seven weeks to do from beginning to end, with longer-term followup as necessary.

Competitive Audit

One effective way of staying in touch with the market is to know what the competition is doing. No one has a better "feel" for the competition than a good field auditor. For a complete picture, the auditor should speak not only with sales personnel, but with the developer of the competing project as well. Both telephone interviews and onsite visits may be used, though an onsite audit offers the added advantage of face-to-face contact (Figure 10).

Absorption

One of the key questions to be answered about the proposed development is how long the absorption period will be. The absorption period refers to the amount of time it will take to sell out or lease up a real estate project.

There are two levels of absorption analysis:

- Total market absorption, which involves a review and reconciliation of supply and demand factors in the market, and
- Site-specific absorption—what is often referred to as market capture.

Total market absorption is, in essence, total effective demand. To determine this, the market researcher first audits competitive supply within the market area. This includes a survey of all competitive projects currently selling, under construction, and proposed. Second, population growth and employment increases are forecast to identify demand. Absorption time is projected by reconciling supply and demand. It estimates how much demand—how many months or years of population and employment growth—is necessary to reach an equilibrium with (or "absorb") total supply.

For example, let us assume that the population within the primary market area is projected to increase by 2,250 persons per year over the next 5 years. If the average number of persons per household is stable at 2.25, then one could assume a demand for 1,000 housing units per year during that time period (excluding allowance for population living in group dwellings, and vacancy rates). The total number of unsold dwelling units that are existing, under construction, and proposed within the same market area is 2,500. Under this scenario, it should take the market approximately 2.5 years to absorb the current supply, assuming newly forming households are the same size as past households. Competitive analysis should provide this information.

This is a general analysis. A more specific delineation of supply and demand will be helpful. For example, what portion of total supply is comparable in price and function to your product? What portion of demand wants a home in this price range and function? In other words, can you clearly define the demand from your market?

Why is absorption so important? Because it affects the bottom line. Given the cost of construction financing, the absorption time becomes critical to success or failure. A development that is profitable if sold out in 18 months may be a loser if it takes 3 years to sell out.

The second level of absorption analysis, market capture, evaluates the subject site in terms of its capture of projected demand. It is at this level of analysis where the value of market research becomes most evident.

The site's percentage capture within a given area reflects how well the project is suited for, and marketed to that marketplace. The market research identifies market segments, consumer preferences, effective advertising and merchandising techniques, proper pricing, and other items. Projected market capture is an assessment of how the development plan at the subject site relates to these factors. Obviously, those projects that are better suited for the marketplace should realize stronger sales.

A good basis for determining market capture may begin with a "fair share" analysis of the market. Determine the number of competing projects that are likely to be marketing homes (try to be specific to your market— attached, detached, or rental), and divide into total demand for this type of housing. The result shows the fair share capture of each project competing in the market. As a cross reference, compare this number with the absorption rate of product now in the market. If the numbers correspond, the market may be stable and homogeneous. Variations may indicate changing supply/demand factors or a variety of product quality in the marketplace. Fair share calculations can be compared with the current and past market performance of competing product.

Figure 10. Sample Competitive Audit Form

Audit Date
4/10/86

Project Name
LOMAS SERENAS

Developer/Builder
LOMAS SANTA FE, INCORPORATED

Product Type
Detached

Sales Organization
LOMAS SANTA FE, INCORPORATED

Lot Characteristics
20,000 SQUARE FOOT MINIMUM

Engineer
N.A.

Architect
NAEGLE ASSOCIATES, INCORPORATED

Location
WEST I-15 ON VIA RANCHO PARKWAY

Sales Office Phone #
(619) 587-1455

Interior Designer
R. CARLISLE

Construction Lender
N.A.

Project #: **4192**

Market Area
Escondido

Map #
THOMAS BROTHERS 27 E/3

Data Opened
3/31/79

Model Merchandising
6 FULLY FURNISHED

Plans	Bed/Bath	Square Foot	Stories	Overall Units Avail.	Overall Unit Sold	Monthly Units Avail.	Monthly Unit Sold	Current Base Price	Prior Base Price	Date of Last Change	Premium to:	Current Price per Square Foot
6	3/2.50	2232	1	24	22	2	0	199,000	203,000	9/06/85	33,000	89.15
7	3/2.50	2502	1	13	13	0	0	Sold Out	217,000	12/05/85	8,000	
8	4/3.00	2708	2	18	16	5	3	239,000	225,000	3/12/86	10,000	88.25
9	4/2.50	2841	1	23	21	2	0	255,000	245,000	3/12/86	10,000	89.75
13	5/2.50	3195	1	25	23	2	0	285,000	275,000	12/05/85	10,000	89.20
22	4/3.00	2875	2	8	8	0	0	285,000	276,000	3/12/86		99.13
5	4/3.00	2299	2	8	6	3	1	222,000	225,000	1/09/86	17,000	96.56

FINANCING

Down	Interest	Loan Type
MARKET	CONV.	

FINANCING NOTES

NO SPECIAL FINANCING OFFERED.

	Current Month 4/10/86	Last Month 3/12/86	Total Project 3/31/79
Total Sales	4	3	220
Sales per Week	.96	.61	.60
Escrows Closed	2	1	201

INSITES ™

SUBDIVISION FEATURES

Maintenance Fee: **$25.00 / QUARTER ***

Pool	Sauna	Spa
Rec. Room	Tennis	Putting Green

Security

***FEE COVERS ROOF INS.& STREET UPKEEP**

Driveway **ASPHALT**

Parking **3 CAR GARAGE**

Fencing Height **NONE**

Landscaping **NONE**

Balcony: **NO**   Patio: **NO**

Roof Type:

Utility Room Location **IN HOUSE**

Washer/Dryer **NONE**

Walk-in Closet: **MASTER OTHER**

Flooring **CRPTS/TILE ENT. & KIT.**

Luminous Lighting: **KITCHEN BATH**

Heating: **F/A** Air Cond. **INCLUDED**

Tub Type and Surrounding **PORC/CERAMIC TILE**

Shower **TILE**

Pullman Tops **CERAMIC TILE**

Counter Tops **CERAMIC TILE**

Pantry **CUPBOARD**

Sinks **DBL/PORCELAIN**

Oven Brand of Type **G.E./SGL/ELC/S.C.**

Microwave: **OPTIONAL**

Dishwasher Brand or Cycle **G.E./2 CYCLE**

Fireplace **WOODBURNING**

Wet Bar: **YES** Drapes: **NO**

TRASH COMPACTOR. GARAGE DOOR OPENER.
SPA TUB IN MASTER BATH. G.E. COOK
TOP. CENTRAL VACUUM OPTIONAL.
SKYLIGHTED ENTRY PLANS 8 & 9.
PLAN 7&9 OPTIONAL DEN,
PLANS 7&9 FAM ROOM. G.E. COOKTOP.

SUBDIVISION ACTIVITY

Development Size **306**
Acreage

Tract/Unit Filing Number	Number Built	Under Const.	Approved	Planned	Sales Started	Number Sold	Standing Inventory
9064/1-4	111				3/31/79	111	
9064/V	19				9/01/83	19	
9064/VI	22				12/01/83	22	
9064/VII	13				6/01/84	13	
9064/VIII	21				11/01/84	21	
MODELS	6				NOT RELEASED		6
9064/IX	25				5/15/85	19	6
9064/X		19			12/14/85	15	4
Total	217	19				220	16

BUYER PROFILE

Singles	
Single w/c	10%
Young Couple w/c	70%
Young Couple wo/c	
Couples w/teens	10%
Empty Nester	5%
Retirees	
Investors	5%

Area Previously Lived In **OUT OF TOWN/LOCAL**

Area Working In **LOCAL/SAN DIEGO/SAN MARCOS**

ADVERTISING/TRAFFIC

Newspapers	30%	TV	
Magazine	10%	Signs	45%
Radio		Other	15%

ADVERTISING NOTES

HOMES FOR SALE AND THE SAN DIEGO UNION
OTHER=REFERRAL
LOCAL PAPERS SPOT BASIS

ADDITIONAL NOTES

CUMULATIVE MIX BEGINS WITH PHASE V.
REMAINING INVENTORY: PHASE IX - PLAN 5:2, PLAN 6:1, PLAN 8:3,
                      PLAN 9:1, PLAN 13:1.
                      PHASE X - PLAN 6:1, PLAN 8:1, PLAN 9:1,
                      PLAN 13:1.
MODELS: PLANS 5, 6, 7, 8, 9 & 13
SALES REP: "LIZ" (619) 587-1455

The Goodkin Group

Conclusion

In summary, market research can reduce the risk inherent in real estate development. It takes time and discipline. However, absolute dollar investment may be only $5.00 to $25.00 per unit, depending on the scope of the research and project size. This is not a high price to pay to target your market. If managed properly, market research can be of assistance during the development process from project conception to closing the last escrow.

Market research is being used more and more frequently. Lenders are increasingly motivated to require market and site feasibility research and analysis for projects that they fund with construction and take-out loans. Builders see a changing market with increased and more sophisticated competition, as well as changing economics and demographics.

Finally, opportunities for market research are increasing. The increasing availability of information from a variety of sources allows a more refined analysis of the housing consumer. This creates opportunity for better design and more effective, efficient communication with target markets. The result: lower costs and increased profits.

3. Approval Process

The planning, zoning, and subdivision process that has evolved over the past several decades is geared primarily toward conventional single-family detached development. It includes such traditional elements as standard lot sizes, setbacks, rights-of-way, and single purpose land use districts.

Some local government policy makers view higher density housing as a transitional use between single-family neighborhoods and commercial and industrial land uses. Zoning regulations often relegate higher density developments to sites along major highways. As a result, these developments are not considered an integral part of the community. Where higher density development is permitted, local governments have established elaborate review and approval systems to soften the perceived impact of higher density on the community. The criteria they establish often contain standards that are more stringent than those applied to so-called conventional development.

Problems Builder/Developers Face

The evolution of contemporary zoning methods such as planned unit development (PUD) and clustering has done much to encourage higher density single-family development and to encourage design quality within such projects. Many jurisdictions still do not distinguish between single-family attached and multifamily housing, however. This lack of distinction frequently causes confusion and misinterpretation of what a particular project will look like and what its impact will be on the community.

It is not uncommon for local governments to apply traditional "multifamily" zoning regulations to higher density development. These regulations, which originated during the post-World War II years, mandate parcel sizes for multifamily structures, precise building configurations, and restrictive setbacks to building property lines and separations between buildings.

Jurisdictions should be urged to classify townhouses and other forms of attached units as single-family attached land uses. This tends to minimize opposition to such projects, which local residents would otherwise consider to be just another form of garden apartments. Many communities are now creating zones which make this important distinction between single-family attached and true multifamily.

In addition to onerous regulations, builders undertaking higher density developments are frequently subjected to a time-consuming and expensive rezoning, special exception, or conditional use process that often stimulates citizen opposition. When local officials ask why builders do not use innovative methods such as PUD and clustering, builders point to the delays, additional costs, and the exactions—dedications, fees, construction of public facilities—that are involved in gaining approvals for these types of developments. A consistent, predictable approval process would encourage builder/developers to use innovative development techniques.

Local development ordinances with provisions for development techniques such as PUD and clustering often begin with a preamble describing the advantage of these types of development to the community, the environment, and the buyer. Unfortunately, the benefits of these creative techniques are often stymied by the regulations set up to administer them. The benefits to the community would be far greater if innovative planning were promoted in all zones—not just in those which are specifically defined as innovative. The quality of community development would be greatly improved by allowing more options to the developer. Figure 11 shows the type of development that could be achieved if innovative development approaches were permitted by right within any residential zone.

Another common problem builder/developers face is the time it takes to get a higher density project through an often complicated approval system. It is quite common to find a site plan approval requirement added on to the normal process of subdividing the land for higher density development. Public hearing requirements are also common appendages to the site plan approval process. If the hearings are quasi-judicial and require public notice, the process can be delayed for months because of 30-day notification periods. Some communities who find themselves bogged down in a processing bureaucracy have begun to seek alternative approaches to higher density project approval. A few of the more successful alternatives are noted below.

Figure 11. Innovative approaches to higher density development

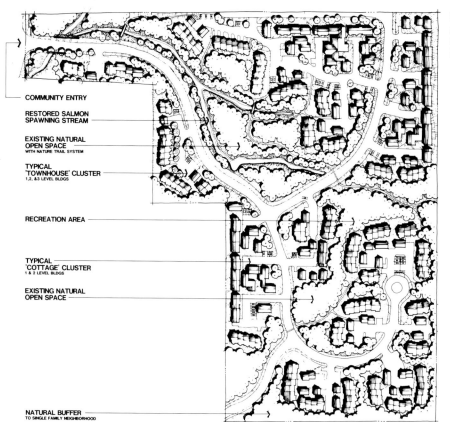

Springbrook Square, Juanita, WA
Architect: Mithun Bowman Emrich
Group, Bellevue, WA
Developer: Conner Development

COMMUNITY ENTRY

RESTORED SALMON
SPAWNING STREAM

EXISTING NATURAL
OPEN SPACE
WITH NATURE TRAIL SYSTEM

TYPICAL
'TOWNHOUSE' CLUSTER
1,2, &3 LEVEL BLDGS

RECREATION AREA

TYPICAL
'COTTAGE' CLUSTER
1 & 2 LEVEL BLDGS

EXISTING NATURAL
OPEN SPACE

NATURAL BUFFER
TO SINGLE FAMILY NEIGHBORHOOD

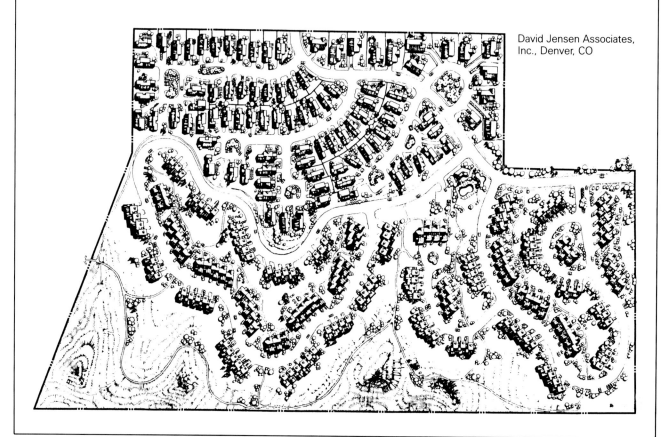

David Jensen Associates,
Inc., Denver, CO

Streamlining the Approval Process

One of the most effective approaches to improving the plan review process is the review committee. Applied at the subdivision review stage, this technique brings together all of the agencies and departments involved in plan review in a meeting with the applicant. In this way, all comments on an application are conveyed to the applicant in person. Conflicts with agency requirements are resolved face-to-face and the applicant leaves the meeting knowing what steps he/she has to take to receive an approval. The review committee cannot resolve all problems in every case; therefore, the planning commission may be called upon to serve as the final arbiter as needed.

Another common streamlining technique is for local government to give the planning director or equivalent personnel the authority for administrative approval without a formal hearing before the planning commission. This technique is especially effective for resubdivisions, revisions to approved plans, and extensions of approval. Since higher density projects are frequently developed in stages, with adaptations to reflect changes in the market, this kind of administrative authority can save many weeks of resubmittal and review.

The two alternatives discussed above apply to subdivision of the land. A third approach, the pre-application conference, can be applied to the subdivision process and site plan review. The purpose of the conference is to give the applicant the opportunity to meet with local plan reviewers prior to making a formal application for project approval, usually for land subdivision. Generally, the procedure helps avoid delays in processing due to incomplete applications, misinterpretation of requirements, and the like. While some communities require the pre-application conference, it is more effectively used at the discretion of the applicant, who assumes any risks associated with eliminating this step in the process.

It is not uncommon to find communities that permit the applicant to submit site plans concurrently with the subdivision plan. Of course, the applicant is taking a calculated risk that approval will be granted to both portions of the application, and that there will be minimal changes. Pre-application conferences can help to avoid such problems before they arise.

Another approach is for local government to allow the subdivision plan and the site plan to be essentially the same document. In the case of cluster subdivisions, for example, the subdivision plan can also be the site plan. In order for the local jurisdiction to maintain control, compliance is monitored through the building permit process. This procedure can save several weeks of duplicative review.

Still another method is for the city to hire competent, professional planning staff who will work with applicants to achieve their mutual goal of quality development. As with administrative approval, dis-agreements can be resolved by the designated planning authority. This approach assumes that the local community has adopted a positive attitude toward development and that builder/developers are considered an integral part of the process.

To implement the streamlining methods described above, builder/developers must establish good lines of communication with local officials. Many issues that appear controversial at first can be resolved by healthy give-and-take from all parties involved.

The Role of Local Government

Local government can play a major role in solving approval problems. Municipalities and counties must recognize the advantages of planning for a variety of housing types and densities when preparing their comprehensive plans and land development regulations. Local governments should designate where and when they can accommodate higher density. They should even go one step further by prezoning areas for higher density development rather than subjecting the builder/developer to the difficult rezoning process. This enables both builder/developers and the general public to know where higher densities are permitted.

In reality, though, even prezoning will not always reduce processing time. For example, if only a small area is designated for higher density development, inflated land values could cause builder/developers to seek rezonings in other areas of the community.

Capital Improvements Plan

Planning for a variety of housing types and densities can be supported through a municipal capital improvements plan (CIP). A CIP is a schedule for the provision of capital improvements over a specified period of time. It is a proven and accepted method used by governments to plan for improvements such as utilities, schools, parks, and roads. The improvement items are listed in order of priority, and are accompanied by specific cost estimates and a source of financing for each item. Most municipal budgets provide only for those improvements which will be begun or completed within that fiscal year.

Many communities are currently exploring ways to assess new development for capital improvement costs. Cuts in federal assistance have motivated local governments to seek alternative sources of financing. Where local tax increases are unworkable, many communities are turning to impact fees, tax increment financing districts, and other revenue producers. This is popular with existing residents, but places an undue burden upon new residents who have no voice in the decision-making process.

Alternative Approaches to Zoning

While examples of progressive tools such as PUD and clustering have been cited, the use of more conventional zoning tools can still encourage flexibility and innovation in project design. Zoning ordinances frequently establish densities through minimum lot size rather than through the number of dwelling units, or people, per acre. An alternative to allowing PUD-like flexibility within all zones would be to establish a maximum allowable density without predetermining minimum lot sizes. A much greater degree of design flexibility within conventional zones would result. Such a system would allow the builder/developer to cluster or provide a variety of lot sizes without going through a complicated permit process. The community would retain control over the density level, but would not restrict the designs used to achieve it.

Under this system, the conventional subdivision plat review procedure remains in place, allowing the community to monitor the development of lots within its boundaries. This approach has been applied in some communities in Florida and appears to be working well.

Coordination of Regulations

In addition to reexamining the substance of development regulations, better coordination among review agencies and their respective regulations is needed. Many problems arise over road frontage, utility, or safety standards that are enforced by the local engineering or public works department but conflict with planning department regulations.

For example, conflicts have occurred between a state's condominium, cooperative, or horizontal property laws and local zoning and subdivision codes. Due to minimum lot size or road frontage regulations, a locality may force a builder/developer to develop a condominium project rather than a fee-simple subdivision. The result may be several months of delay due to state laws governing the formation of a condominium association.

As another example, zoning regulations that permit zero lot line houses can be undermined by engineering standards that deal with fire safety and separation of units. The result: some communities either prohibit zero lot line development or regulate it heavily. In fact, however, the distance between homes in a zero lot line development and a conventional development may be the same—a point which local regulatory agencies should understand.

A project in Las Vegas encountered this problem. Simple interpretation and clarification of the codes could have eliminated the requirement to add parapets for so-called fire protection. Had the houses been located five feet off the lot line, maintaining the same distance between units, the parapets would not have been required.

A final example of the need for regulatory coordination is found in the efforts of local planning agencies to limit the amount of grading on a higher density site. Local grading regulations commonly require more grading than the builder/developer or the planning agency would like. Again, simple coordination and communication can remove such obstacles.

Conclusion

This chapter has focused on problems that builders and developers confront when seeking approvals for higher density projects. The approval process for higher density housing should parallel that required for traditional, low density single-family developments. It is the responsibility of local government to plan for a wide variety of housing types and to ensure that the approval process does not undercut housing goals. This will require:

- Streamlined processing techniques
- New attitudes toward higher density development and its benefits to the community
- The application of new and imaginative techniques for protecting community health, safety, and public welfare

Design

Figure 12. Planned unit developments (PUDs)

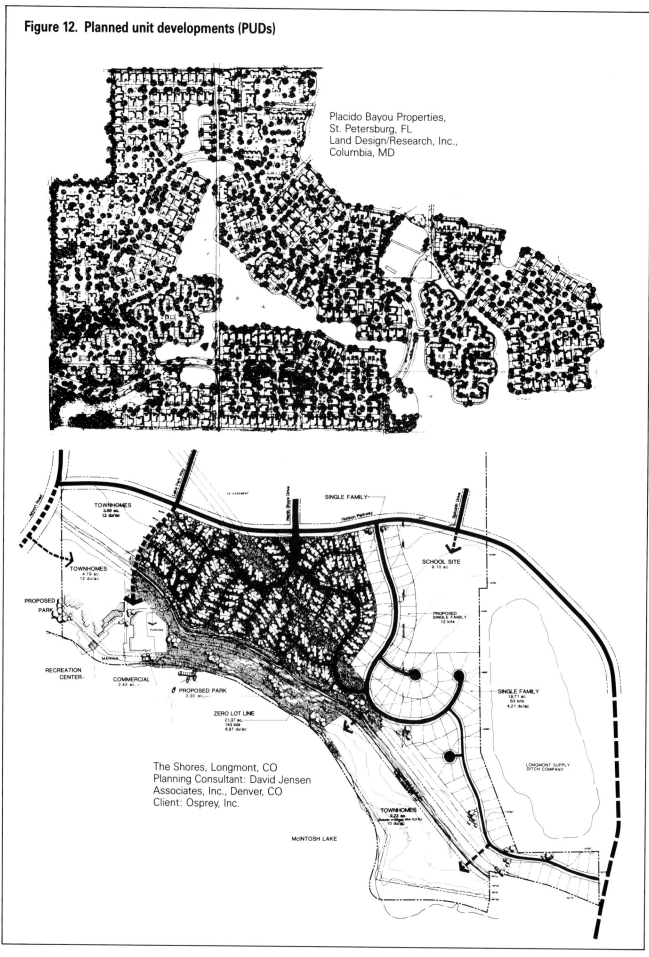

Placido Bayou Properties,
St. Petersburg, FL
Land Design/Research, Inc.,
Columbia, MD

The Shores, Longmont, CO
Planning Consultant: David Jensen
Associates, Inc., Denver, CO
Client: Osprey, Inc.

1. Introduction

The development of higher density communities requires a more sensitive design approach than is generally found in traditional detached housing. At higher densities, individual homes become an integral feature of the overall project plan, and the project itself interacts to a greater degree with the larger community. In order to maximize the assets of higher density development, builders should understand the importance of the design relationships between community, project, and unit.

Higher density development offers an increased perception of security, controlled traffic flow, more affordable housing, and exciting living environments. While local market conditions determine the specific design approach and construction techniques for a particular project, some general guidelines apply in the planning and design of higher density housing. The chapters that follow discuss these general rules, identify some of the challenges of designing higher density projects, and suggest solutions to these challenges.

Approaches to Higher Density Development

The planned unit development (PUD) is a development technique that allows the implementation of land designs which fit the market, the site, and the community. The concept permits mixing of residential and commercial uses, usually at increased density and intensity (Figure 12). The use of PUD usually requires a zoning change; it can also be a conditional use within designated zones or can be implemented as a "floating zone."

The advantages of PUD include the preservation of open space and natural features, reduced land development costs, flexibility in processing, and most importantly, flexibility in design standards. Standards existing within conventional zones are waived in favor of standards proposed by the developer to fit the image and need of the particular project.

With PUDs, the concept of clustering is frequently applied. Although it can be used independently of the PUD, clustering provides the means to reduce the developed area of the site by creating more compact groups or clusters of units and lots, both attached and detached. Clustering shares with PUD the concept of flexible design standards established to fit the site, project, and market.

Like the PUD concept, cluster results in reduced land development costs, as development is concentrated and open spaces and natural features are preserved. Unlike PUD, clustering usually provides no increase in gross density but does increase permitted net densities. It also allows for the mixing of attached and detached units within the same site. In terms of plan processing, cluster is most efficient if it is permitted as a development option within designated residential zones.

Figure 13. Entrances designed for maximum visual impact

Community/project entrance

Spring Lane Condominiums, Salt Lake City, UT
Spring Lane Building Associates
Photography: Robb Miller

Individual unit entrance

La Vita, Altamonte Springs, FL
Danielian Associates Architects/Planners, Newport Beach, CA

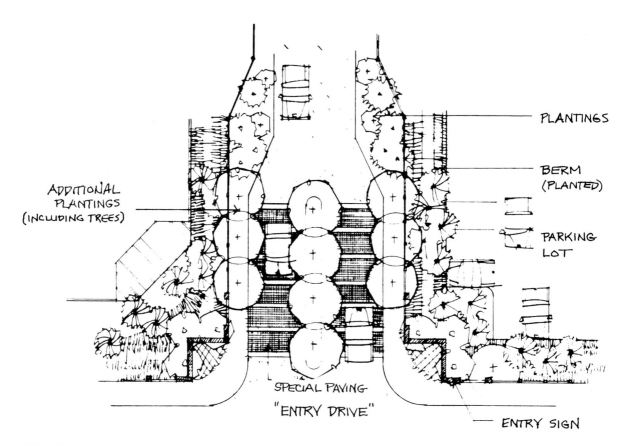

Street/cluster entrance

David Jensen Associates, Inc., Denver, CO

2. The Design Program

Levels of Design

While project densities vary with market demand, the design program for any higher density project should consider three "layers" of design impact (Figure 13):

- Community/project entrance
- Street/cluster entrance
- Individual unit entrance

The project entry, street layout, the interaction between buildings and open space, and the distinction between individual units all set the stage for the final arrival into the unit itself. The buyer's initial impression of the unit can make or break a project. The power of a dramatic entry, no matter what the price range of the project, colors the buyer's perception of both the entire development and the individual unit. Specific design approaches are discussed later in this chapter.

After conducting the necessary market research to determine a project's market segment, as discussed in the Planning section, the builder must establish a consistent theme or concept to guide project design and development. This theme should be utilized throughout the entire design/arrival/perception process (Figure 14). The theme helps to let prospective buyers know the range and type of project amenities that are available. Inconsistent themes can result in missed messages, missed markets, and missed sales opportunities.

As prospective home buyers advance from project entry to the unit, they should perceive a series of cues that communicate a consistent message of *arrival* and *home*. Serial cues work on two levels: psychological and perceptual.

Psychological cues influence the buyer's sense of arrival, awareness of neighborhoods, and the overall sense of community scale. Entrance treatment, ease of movement through the project, and clear neighborhood identification are good examples of psychological cues that communicate well to the potential buyer (Figure 15).

Color, texture, landscaping, window and entry details are perceptual cues that influence how the buyer "sees" the project at close range (Figure 16).

Such perceptual cues highlight identity and character at the individual building or unit level, and help complete the perception of *arrival* and *home*. The builder/developer should follow through on these cues to ensure the successful presentation of the project's theme.

Putting the Team Together

Builder/developers undertaking higher density housing for the first time should consult with experts who have previously designed and marketed these types of projects. Reliance on expert advice early in the planning process helps to ensure sound results. It is also a good idea to visit several existing projects to learn how other builder/developers, planners, and designers have approached similar types of projects. Successful community developments demonstrate the value of careful attention to detail. They prove the value of a simple, well-developed design that is evident throughout the site plan, individual floor plans, and in the marketing effort.

The builder/developer should bring together all major contributors to the design team early in the planning process. The team could consist of a market research/marketing specialist, a land planner, an architect, a site engineer, and a landscape architect. The actual team profile can vary when professionals with multiple talents are employed; the list above simply includes those that are most commonly used. Each of these professionals brings a unique talent to the project development team.

Armed with market research data and an understanding of the target market, the architect, land planner, market researcher/marketing consultant, and builder/developer should discuss how the elements of the project will fit together. Design, theme selection, site construction techniques, marketing, and product presentation are all interrelated. Discussions among all team members in the planning stages can highlight areas that may need special attention.

Decision making in the planning of conventional lower density development has traditionally not required close coordination between professionals. Lots were big enough to accommodate many different types and shapes of unit designs. Higher density, on the other hand, demands a much closer degree of coordination between land plan and unit designs. In attached and stacked building units, for example, construction details that emphasize individual unit identity but relate to the theme of the community can be as important as the overall project design. Further, the builder/developer's input at the planning stage can simplify the construction process by identifying the need for modified details, more cost-effective materials, or clearer construction drawings.

Figure 14. Nautical project theme

The Boatyard, Falmouth, MA
Bloodgood Architects, P.C., Des Moines, IA
Land Planner: Matarazzo Design,
Concord, NH
Photography: Phokion Karas

Figure 15. Psychological cues communicate project theme through a sense of overall community scale and neighborhood identification

The Park at Southern Hills, Des Moines, IA
Bloodgood Architects, P.C., Des Moines, IA
Photography: Hedrich Blessing

Figure 16. Perceptual cues express project theme at close range

Pentridge Cove, Costa Mesa, CA
Danielian Associates Architects/
Planners, Newport Beach, CA

3. Higher Density Housing Types

Single-Family Detached

Conventional Development

The tradition of the single-family detached home is strong and is likely to remain the preferred house type among the nation's home buyers. The conventional single-family house is sited on its own lot in accordance with development regulations that prescribe front, side and rear yard dimensions. Frequently, however, the yard area is broken up, limiting its usefulness for outdoor activities. The inefficiency of this type of lot is particularly apparent in the narrow side yards.

Rising land development costs have driven new home selling prices upward, forcing builder/developers to devise more cost-effective land planning techniques (Figure 17). As available land resources diminish, it is imperative that land be used as efficiently as possible, concentrating growth where public services are available. The relationship of the single-family detached unit to its lot, to other units, and to the larger community must be examined to identify alternative means for using land resources cost-effectively.

Reductions in lot and house size are part of the solution. The zero lot line house, the patio home, and the detached condominium are single-family detached house types that challenge the wisdom and efficiency of the conventional detached house on a large lot.

Zero Lot Line

The zero lot line (ZLL) house is usually a single-family detached unit with one or more exterior walls sited on a lot line. Design techniques include the following:

- Staggered or "z-lot"
- Angled
- Pinwheel clusters
- Square lot
- Semi-attached

The effective use of yard area is an important design element when smaller houses are sited on smaller than conventional lots. This is particularly true of ZLL designs, which allow outside spaces to become an extension of the inside. The side and rear yards can be designed to serve as an additional living area, especially in temperate climates (Figure 18).

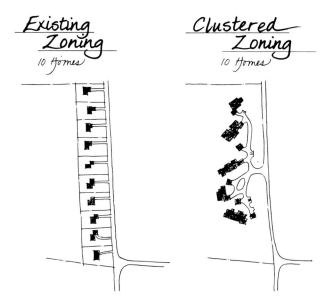

Figure 17. Higher density lot configurations often use land more cost-effectively than does conventional single-family development

Matarazzo Design, Concord, NH

Zero lot line units, regardless of type, can be enhanced by varying the setback of both houses and garages. A repeating setback pattern can create a monotonous streetscape, however, so variations in setbacks must be carefully considered. Special topographic conditions, significant native cover, and unusual natural features offer opportunities to create a range of setbacks and unit orientations along the street. On flat sites with little vegetation, particular attention must be paid to landscaping adjacent to the street. A treeless higher density project will more than likely generate community opposition to future higher density projects. Design quality must be inherent in every application of the higher density concept.

The staggered ("z-lot") design creates unusual

Figure 18. Zero lot line yards can be designed as an extension of interior living space

Sea Cliff, Carlsbad, CA
Architect: Richardson Nagy Martin, Newport Beach, CA
Client: California Communities

Summerwind, Corona del Mar, CA
Kermit Dorius FAIA Architects and Associates, Corona del Mar, CA
Client: Gfeller

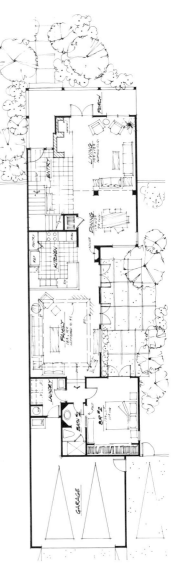

spaces between units and provides the opportunity to integrate a unit's interior and exterior spaces. Staggered lots yield a density of 7-8 units per acre (Figure 19).

Angled zero lot line units are another alternative that provide a varied street scene by eliminating the repetitive pattern of uniform setbacks (Figure 20). Angled lots also allow for a more varied treatment of garages and parking areas, enabling cars to enter the garage from either the side or front. Frequently, however, local subdivision regulations require all lot lines to be perpendicular to the street right-of-way line, although there is no rationale for such a requirement.

One minor drawback of angled lots is residual land at the corners and rear of such lots. There is some disagreement over appropriate design treatment for these areas. If possible, the residual land should be included in the nearest adjacent lot to avoid the maintenance problem associated with commonly owned but noncontiguous parcels (Figure 21). In any

case, these areas should be landscaped and the units carefully sited to maximize use of the space. The density per acre of angled units ranges from 6.8-7.8.

Pinwheel clusters of zero lot line units are a third design alternative. Called pinwheels because their site plan layout resembles a pinwheel fan, these units increase the normal ZLL density to 8-12 units per acre. This increase is achieved by a trade-off in the parking design, however. As shown in Figure 22, parking for pinwheels is located in compounds rather than with individual units. Buyers in some markets may not accept this concept, so developers planning pinwheel clusters should be sure to identify the preferences of potential buyers through market research.

The pinwheel concept gives each unit a private yard which is isolated from the other three units in the group. A cluster or village atmosphere can be created when densities are pushed to 12 units per acre. As in any higher density project, it is important to remember that small design details become more

Figure 19. Staggered ("z-lot") zero lot line

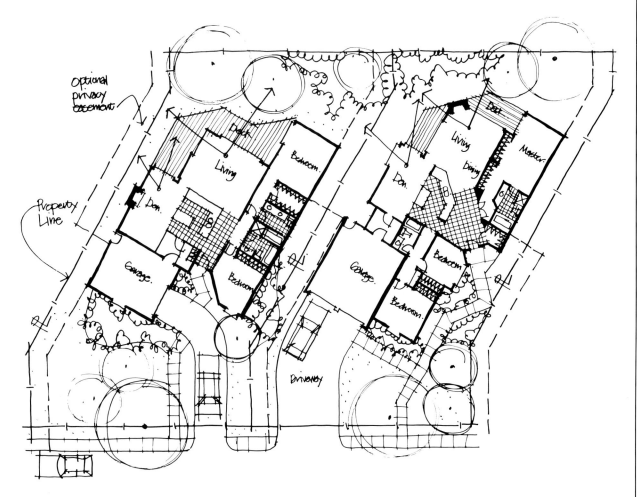

The Martin Organization, Philadelphia, PA

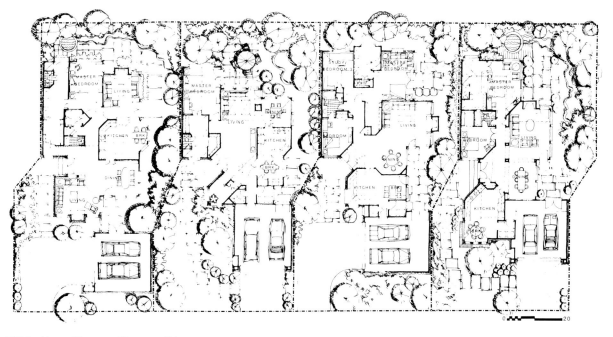

EDI Architects/Planners, Houston, TX

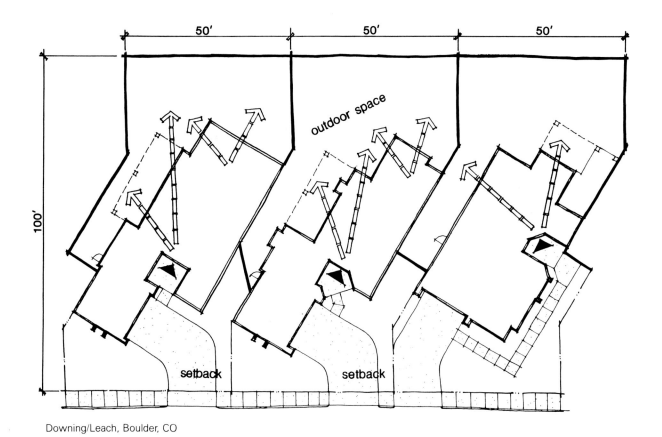

Downing/Leach, Boulder, CO

Figure 20. Angled zero lot line

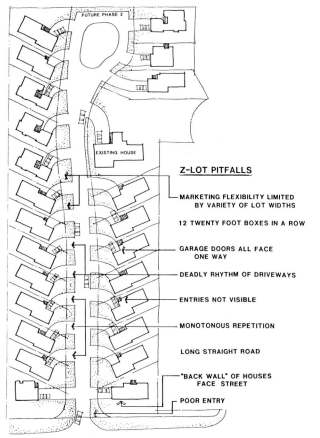

Z-LOT PITFALLS

MARKETING FLEXIBILITY LIMITED BY VARIETY OF LOT WIDTHS

12 TWENTY FOOT BOXES IN A ROW

GARAGE DOORS ALL FACE ONE WAY

DEADLY RHYTHM OF DRIVEWAYS

ENTRIES NOT VISIBLE

MONOTONOUS REPETITION

LONG STRAIGHT ROAD

"BACK WALL" OF HOUSES FACE STREET

POOR ENTRY

PRELIMINARY PLAT

EXISTING STRUCTURE USED AS RECREATION BUILDING

IMPROVED STREETSCAPE

UNIFORM LOT WIDTH ALLOWS ANY MODEL TO FIT ANY SITE FOR MARKETING FLEXIBILITY AND VISUAL VARIETY

ENTRIES ALL FACE STREET

ALTERNATE VISIBILITY OF GARAGE DOORS

PAIRED DRIVEWAYS MAXIMIZES LANDSCAPING, ALLOWS LANDSCAPING TO SOFTEN STRAIGHT ROAD

STRONG ENTRY

ANGLE OF HOUSES INVITES ENTRY

GENEROUS LANDSCAPED SPACE

FINAL PLAT

Mithun Bowman Emrich Group, Bellevue, WA

Figure 21. Angled zero lot line: effective use of residual land

The Berkus Group, Santa Barbara, CA

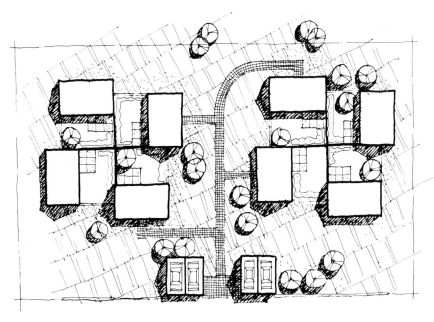

Figure 22. Pinwheel-cluster zero lot line

Mithun Bowman Emrich Group, Bellevue, WA

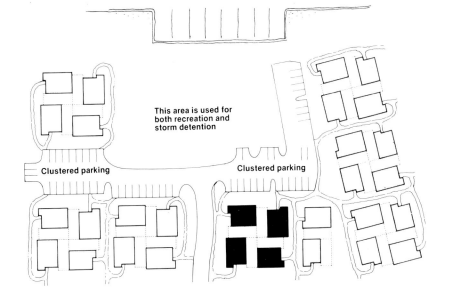

This area is used for both recreation and storm detention

Clustered parking

Clustered parking

The Cottages, Lacey, WA
Designer/Builder: Phillips Homes, Olympia, WA
Planning Consultant: David Clinger and Associates, Lookout Mountain, CO
American Planning Association

Figure 23. Square zero lot line

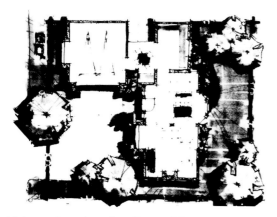

David Jensen Associates, Inc., Denver, CO

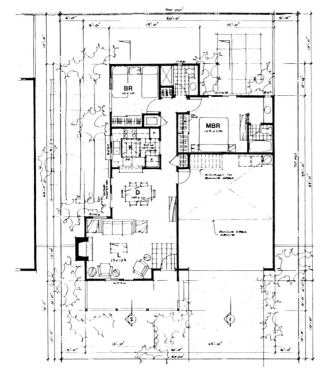

The Bungalows, Valencia, CA
Kermit Dorius FAIA Architects and Associates, Corona del Mar, CA
Client: The Valencia Company

significant when units are smaller and closer together. Window locations, placement of air conditioning units, trash collection, roof designs, and types and colors of materials must be carefully planned in a pinwheel cluster.

The *square lot* ZLL, a variation of the pinwheel, is also possible (Figure 23). Densities of 8-12 units per acre can be achieved using the square lot, and parking is usually provided in bays rather than individual spaces, garages, or carports.

Units can also be *semi-attached* at the rear or side by garages, arbors, or porticos, at a density of 8-12 units per acre. Community zoning regulations will determine the extent to which these attachments may be permitted. Although it is common to find

prohibitions on the use of attached ZLL units, some local regulations have begun to allow the flexibility of using such designs (which are then subject to a site plan review).

All of the methods described above offer distinct advantages over conventional siting techniques. A mix of techniques may be used within a single project, although the appropriateness of each method depends upon site conditions and the preferences of the target market.

It is important to note that some communities do not have provisions for zero lot line development. However, this problem can be overcome by granting use easements for the zero lot line yard (Figure 24). If it is not possible to incorporate ZLL by right within the local zoning code, the easement is an acceptable alternative. Many of the ZLL variations discussed above can be achieved through the easement process, simply by recording the easement on each lot as desired. A potential drawback to this alternative may be buyer resistance to the easement concept.

Patio Homes

Patio homes are well suited to either conventional single-family detached or zero lot line development. They are designed to bring outdoor living space close to high activity areas inside the house. The siting of patio homes takes advantage of maximum sun exposure and provides an extension of the interior living space. The units are often, but not always, one story. Density for patio homes can range from 5-10 units per acre (Figure 25).

Patio homes are particularly appropriate in warm weather climates, since they enable homeowners to enjoy outdoor living during much of the year. Assuring each unit's privacy makes the placement of the house on its site a critical design decision. While the design of the unit itself enhances the sense of privacy, site orientation is the most important consideration in developing patio homes.

Parking for the patio home is typically accommodated on the lot. Other options such as clustered auto courts can also be used.

Detached Condominiums

Condominium ownership is generally thought of in terms of multifamily apartments or single-family attached units. However, single-family detached condominiums are also possible. Since the condominium is simply a form of ownership and not a unit type, its use is not restricted to attached or multifamily uses. A single-family detached condominium operates in the same fashion as the more familiar condominium apartments and townhouses. Each unit and the ground on which it sits is individually owned, while most of the yard area and all common open space is owned by the condominium association set up to maintain it (Figure 26).

Figure 24. Use easement for zero lot line development

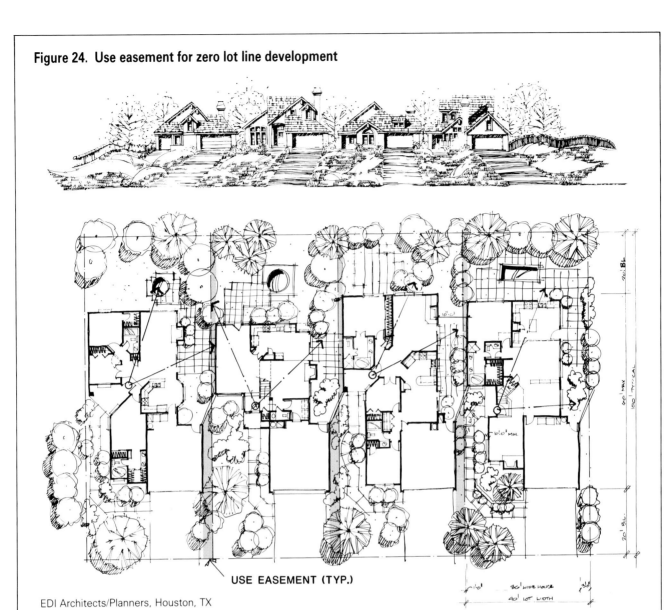

USE EASEMENT (TYP.)

EDI Architects/Planners, Houston, TX

Figure 25. Patio homes offer expanded opportunities for indoor/outdoor living

Monterrey Court, Columbia, MD
Land Design/Research, Inc., Columbia, MD

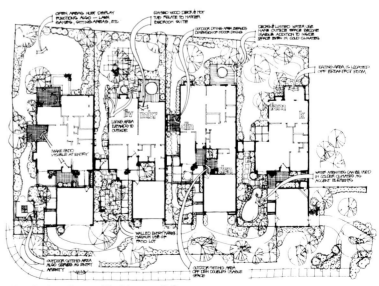

The Berkus Group, Washington, D.C.

Figure 26. Single-family detached condominiums: a form of ownership, not a unit type

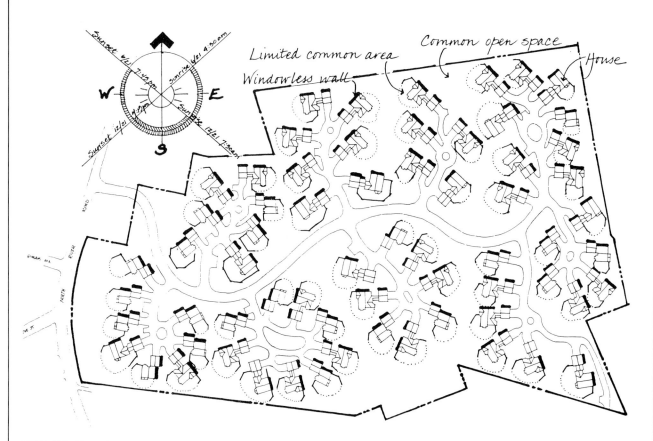

Straw Hill, Manchester, NH
Architect/Land Planner: Matarazzo
Design, Concord, NH
Client: Brownfields Partnership
Photography: Joseph St. Pierre

Single-Family Attached

Single-family attached units lend themselves to any one of four generic forms or combinations of forms: duplexes, triplexes, quadruplexes, and townhouses (rowhouses). Do not let your design creativity be stifled by the broad definitions of these unit types, however. Within the scope of each definition there are multiple options for designing units and placing them on the site. For example, while a quadruplex could be considered a townhouse, this book defines townhouses as more than four units attached in one group. Unit names and definitions will vary according to market, so be careful not to limit your design options.

Traditionally, zoning regulations have restricted residential developments to one housing type per project. Planned unit development (PUD), discussed earlier, offers an alternative to one-type housing projects, but its lengthy and often complicated approval process can undermine the cost savings associated with higher density development. Builders and developers often reject the PUD option because it is expensive, time-consuming and frequently does not yield high enough densities to make it an attractive alternative to conventional development.

Fortunately, developers today are increasingly permitted to mix housing types within a single project without having to go through the PUD process. Cluster development can also provide for a mix of residential uses. Unlike PUD, it normally does not require a rezoning and is an acceptable development option within appropriate residential zones. Mixed use clustering (Figure 27) is becoming more common as communities recognize the need for a wider variety of housing choices.

As new planning concepts are adopted across the country, such as the performance approach to site development standards, the relaxation of regulatory constraints on residential development will signal a significant change in the housing industry.

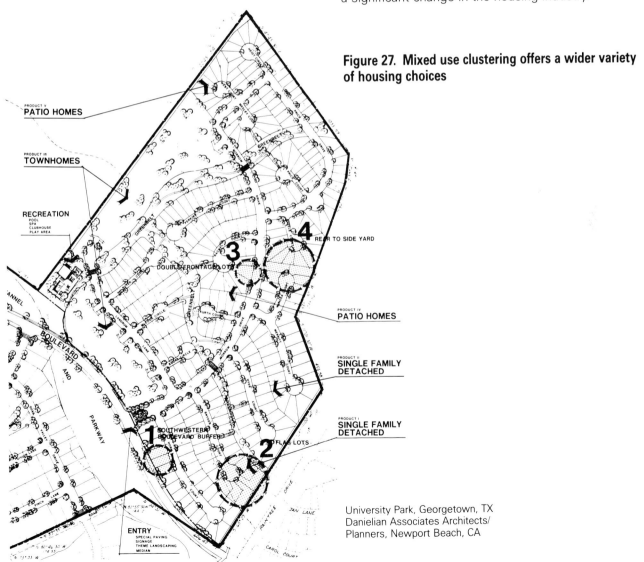

Figure 27. Mixed use clustering offers a wider variety of housing choices

University Park, Georgetown, TX
Danielian Associates Architects/
Planners, Newport Beach, CA

B Unit   A Unit

Figure 28. Duplex designed to look like a pair of townhouses

Indiana Square, Topeka, KS
Planning Consultant: David Jensen Associates, Inc., Denver, CO
Client: Homes by Hogue

Duplexes

The duplex is a single-family attached structure in which two units share a common wall or floor. Duplexes can be designed as side-by-side or back-to-back units. The duplex has traditionally suffered from an image problem as reflected in zoning district provisions. Due to false assumptions that only low-income owners or renters reside in them, duplexes have been considered less desirable than the conventional large, single-family detached home.

Market realities are destroying this myth, however. For example, a duplex may appear to be a pair of townhouses (Figure 28)—a much more "acceptable" housing type in most areas. Combining three or four pairs of duplexes can thus create the same streetscape as a series of townhouses. The density for duplex units can range from 5-6 units per acre up to 10 or more per acre, depending upon site conditions.

The side-by-side unit is the most widely recognized and frequently used duplex type. In the past, entrances have been placed side by side in the front, giving the building a clear identification as a two-family structure (Figure 29). More recently, however, duplex units are being designed to look like a single-family detached house. The effect can be achieved either by placing the entrances on the ends of the units or by orienting one entrance to the street and the other to the side yard. Creative use of building materials, changes in color, and landscaping treatments can produce an attractive structure that conveys a sense of single-family living (Figure 30). Creating a single-family image can offset neighborhood controversy in areas where any form of attached housing is likely to stimulate citizen opposition.

These design approaches are particularly applicable to infill sites within a developed neighborhood. However, many communities have written regulations

Figure 29. Duplex with side-by-side entrances

The Martin Organization, Philadelphia, PA

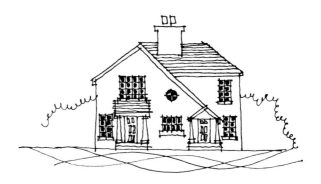

Figure 30. Duplex designed to look like a single-family detached house

The Martin Organization, Philadelphia, PA

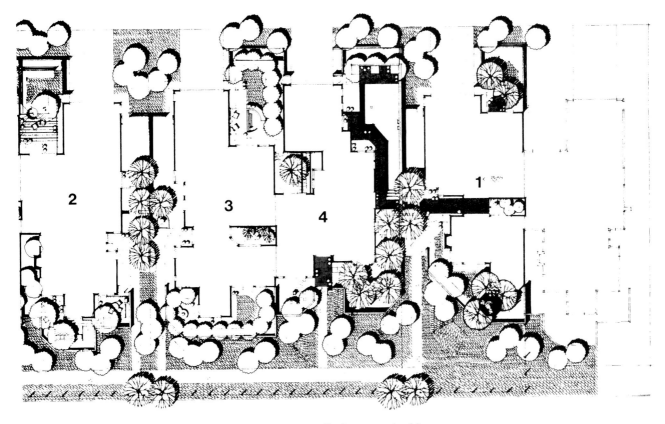

Figure 31. Duplex designed to appear as two separate, distinct attached houses

Danielian Associates Architects/Planners, Newport Beach, CA

prohibiting the use of duplex units on infill sites in response to bad experiences with previous sites or objections from adjacent residents. To minimize community opposition, developers must be careful to address the design details of these types of units.

The duplex unit can also be designed and placed on a site to appear as two distinct attached units (Figure 31). Orientation of entries and garages can be varied depending on the style of the house, site conditions, and the market. Variations in building outline can be achieved through changes in ceiling heights, roof lines, and setbacks, and through other architectural modifications that give each unit its own identity.

Back-to-back duplexes can be thought of as attached zero lot line units, or simply as two units attached at the rear wall, each having a different street or court orientation (Figure 32). A street scene consisting entirely of garage doors can be avoided by using trees and landscaping along driveways. Such plantings visually interrupt the grid and give each unit a distinctive look. The unit facing the public street can be attached to a second unit with access from an alley, auto court, or open space. Roof line, material texture, and color considerations that apply to the conventional duplex are similarly applicable to back-to-back units. Like other attached units, back-to-back duplexes can be mixed with single-family detached

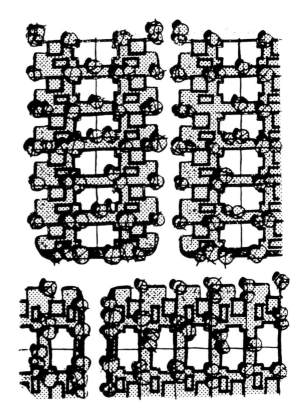

Figure 32. Back-to-back duplexes

The Berkus Group, Santa Barbara, CA

Figure 33. Triplexes

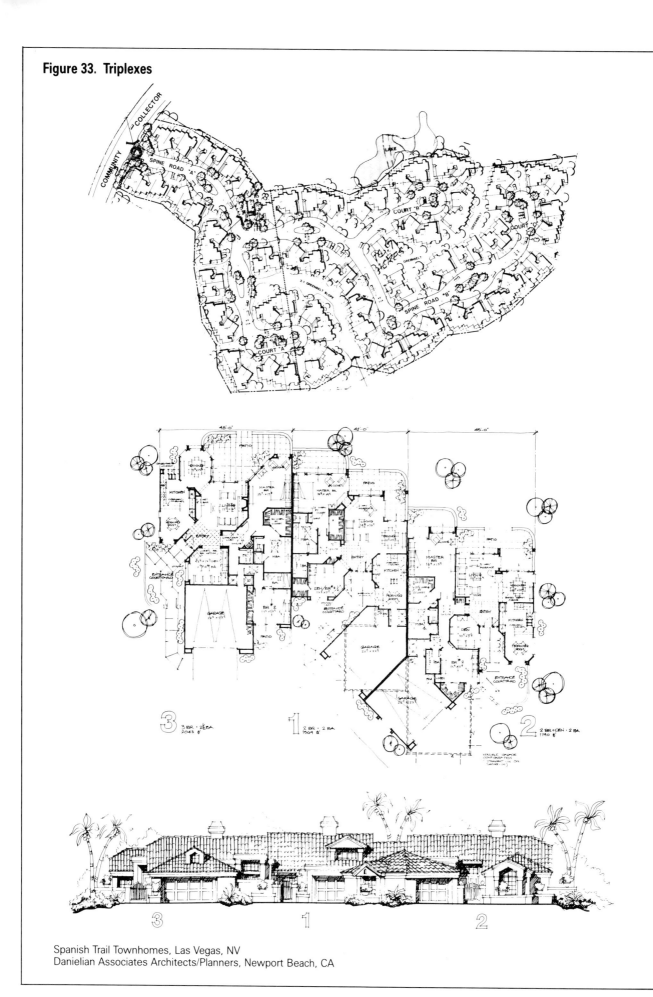

Spanish Trail Townhomes, Las Vegas, NV
Danielian Associates Architects/Planners, Newport Beach, CA

52

homes in clustered or linear arrangements. They can also be used effectively in infill situations.

The over-under duplex, or "two-family unit," as it is commonly referred to in local zoning ordinances, allows the owner to rent out both units or live in one and rent out the other. Often appearing as one unit from the street view, the over-under duplex is actually two living units on a single lot.

Triplexes

The triplex consists of three units attached in a variety of ways (Figure 33). The basic design places the three units side-by-side with varying setbacks, much like conventional townhouse design. Fences, walls, and plant materials may be used to provide visual interest, identity, and a sense of privacy for each unit. Triplex configurations offer the same lifestyle opportunities as do patio homes and duplexes. Combinations of one- and two-story units can provide the design variety that attracts buyers looking for the characteristics of single-family detached units without the price. The degree to which a single-family image is created by the triplex depends upon site conditions, unit design and orientation, and the relationship among units within the project.

The triplex, like the duplex or any of the other attached forms, can be planned in clusters around parking areas or open courts, but can also work well when oriented to the street. Like the duplex, the density of triplexes varies between 6 and 12 units per acre, but can be higher in communities which permit other innovative arrangements in single-family attached projects.

Quadruplexes

The fourplex unit or "quad" is a group of four attached units sited side-by-side, back-to-back in a modified pinwheel around a common axis, or over-under where permitted by the zoning code. Quads can reach densities of 12-14 units per acre or higher depending on site constraints and local zoning provisions.

The most common configuration of the fourplex is the linear arrangement, which provides each unit with its own front and rear yards (Figure 34). In some instances, the units are placed on the front property line, reserving the entire rear area for the yard. Garages, carports, or parking shelters can be placed in front of the units. If the topography is sufficiently variable, parking can be tucked under the unit. It may also be placed in compounds to achieve a higher density.

As an alternative to the more conventional side-by-side layout, quad units can be placed over-under. They can also be designed back-to-back and side-by-side simultaneously. Under this arrangement, each unit maintains its own separate identity with a clearly defined yard area, entrance, parking, and orientation to view. Visual appeal can be achieved through varied roof lines and changes in unit heights from one to two stories. The combination of back-to-back and side-by-side can also create a modified pinwheel effect. Generally, each lot is sold in fee-simple and, as in the zero lot line pinwheel, each unit maintains its privacy (Figure 35).

As with other attached units, the key elements in quad design are adequate access, relationship to other units, the perception of open space, identity, and distance to parking if not provided with each unit. In projects where group parking is provided, the land planner and architect must work together to provide pedestrian access that is efficient without intruding on the privacy of individual units. It should be noted again that there are no limits on creativity in placing these units on the site.

Figure 34. Quadruplex: linear design

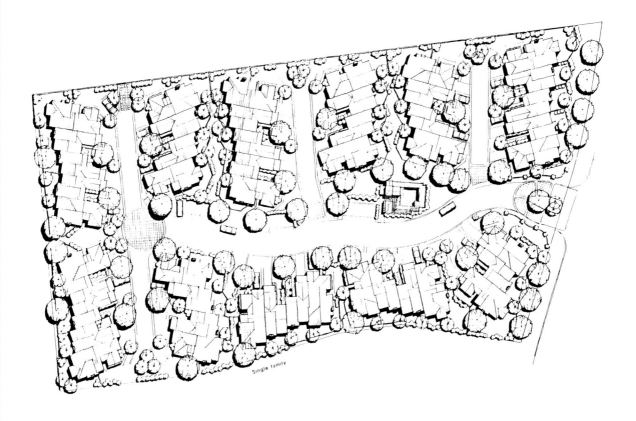

Single family

2   4   3   1

University Park, Georgetown, TX
Downing/Leach, Boulder, CO

54

Figure 35. Quadruplex configurations: Over-under

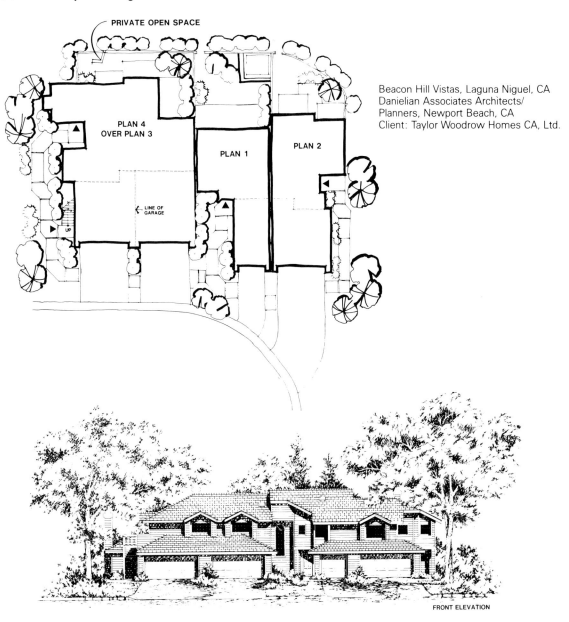

PRIVATE OPEN SPACE

PLAN 4 OVER PLAN 3

PLAN 1

PLAN 2

LINE OF GARAGE

UP

Beacon Hill Vistas, Laguna Niguel, CA
Danielian Associates Architects/
Planners, Newport Beach, CA
Client: Taylor Woodrow Homes CA, Ltd.

FRONT ELEVATION

Back-to-back and side-by-side (modified pinwheel)

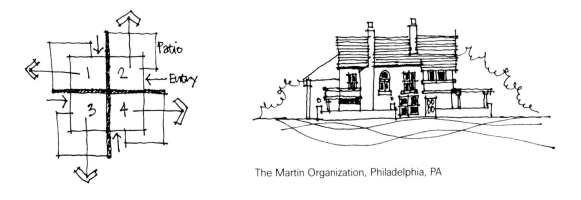

Patio

Entry

1   2

3   4

The Martin Organization, Philadelphia, PA

Townhouses

The townhouse is a single-family attached structure containing five or more units that share one or more wall or floor with an adjoining unit. Like other attached houses, townhouses can be designed and sited to create a broad range of choices for consumers. The most popular attached-unit configuration, townhouses can achieve a density far greater than the usual 10-12 units per acre. Options include the traditional side-by-side or linear arrangement, with common walls at the property lines; L-shaped units and courts; zigzag and staggered units and lots; a back-to-back configuration; and stacked unit arrangements (Figure 36). With the last two options, each unit has at least two walls or floors in common with another unit, and interior units share common walls with three other units. In combination, these configurations have produced densities of up to 30 units per acre.

It is most common to find side-by-side townhouses in the 12-18 units per acre range. Densities can be much higher, however, when local regulations and design standards provide builder/developers with the flexibility to work with the site to achieve high quality higher density products. Imaginative variations on the linear pattern include square, L-shaped, or U-shaped courts that contain parking and open space.

To provide design variety and overcome the monotony of uniform setbacks, townhouses can be staggered or zigzagged along a street or around a court. A more conventional single-family environment can be created by varying the placement of the entry door and garage, and through the liberal use of plant materials. These elements help to reduce building mass and increase privacy. Outdoor space should be considered an additional room, designed to complement the interior layout of the house. Variations in color, texture, roof line, building height, orientation, and view lines should be carefully designed to provide image and identity.

Back-to-back townhouses may be developed at densities not possible with the linear layout. As with zigzag and staggered units, the rear yard is eliminated. Front yards can be owned fee-simple by individual townhouse residents, or maintained as common open space managed by a condominium or homeowners' association. The choice of yard and maintenance options depends on market preference: some buyers desire a yard while others opt for no-maintenance common areas.

The increased density achieved with back-to-back units forces the architect and land planner to make the best possible use of remaining open space by highlighting natural features and adding plant materials where necessary. Existing trees should be saved to provide natural separation between clusters of units. Effective pedestrian and vehicular circulation must also be considered. To the greatest extent possible, vehicular traffic should be separated from unit clusters, and its effect on unit placement kept to a minimum.

Another option is the stacked-unit townhouse, which includes one-over-one, two-over-one, and "wrapped" configurations. Stacked townhouses are popular with buyers who desire one-level living but cannot afford or do not want a single-family detached home. Builder/developers considering stacked units should check local regulations to determine whether stacked townhouses are considered a multifamily use. If so, a rezoning may be required. Additionally, the requirements for parking and open space may differ from those for single-family attached units.

Generally, local codes specify the number of units that may be built contiguously and, sometimes, the degree of setback variation for each unit. Stacked townhouse design must provide for variations in setback in order to give each unit some degree of identity.

Figure 36. Townhouse configurations: Side-by-side or linear

TYPICAL BUILDING

TYPICAL STREET SCENE
4% SLOPE

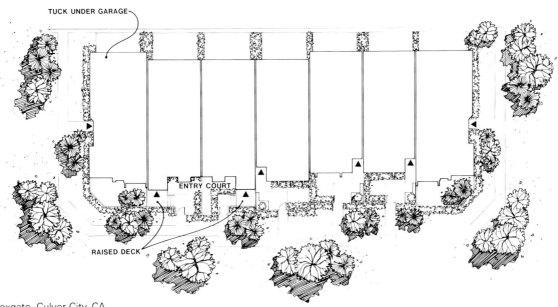

TUCK UNDER GARAGE

ENTRY COURT

RAISED DECK

Foxgate, Culver City, CA
Danielian Associates Architects/Planners, Newport Beach, CA
Client: Bramalea, Ltd.

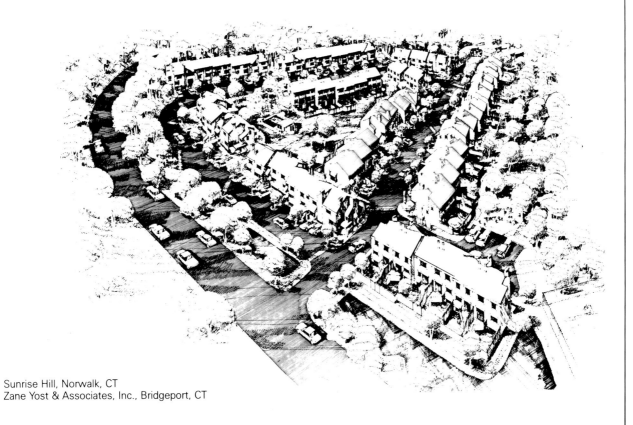

Sunrise Hill, Norwalk, CT
Zane Yost & Associates, Inc., Bridgeport, CT

Townhouse configurations: L-shaped

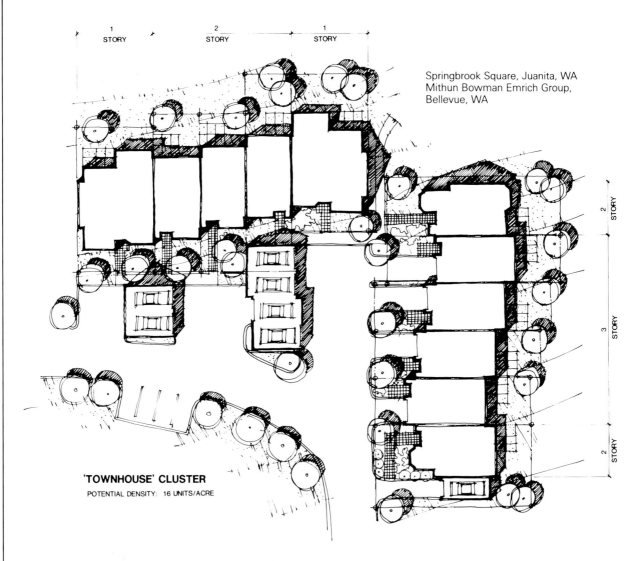

1 STORY 2 STORY 1 STORY

2 STORY

3 STORY

2 STORY

Springbrook Square, Juanita, WA
Mithun Bowman Emrich Group,
Bellevue, WA

'TOWNHOUSE' CLUSTER
POTENTIAL DENSITY: 16 UNITS/ACRE

Cobblestone, Des Moines, IA
Bloodgood Architects, P.C., Des Moines, IA
Builder: Colby Interests, Inc.
Photography: Hedrich Blessing

Townhouse configurations: Mix of staggered and zigzag lots

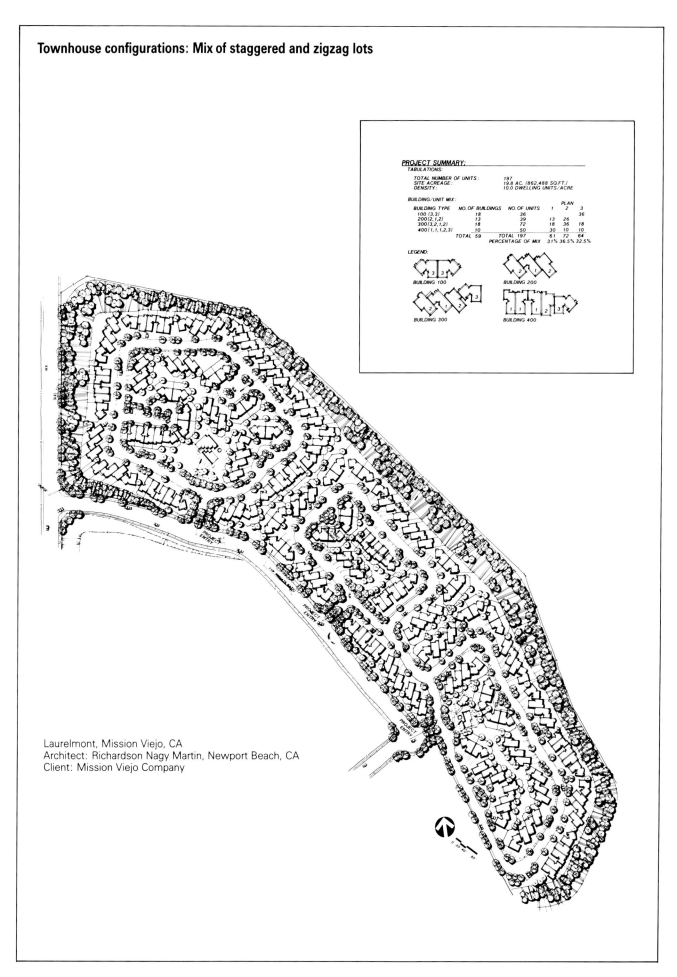

PROJECT SUMMARY:
TABULATIONS:

TOTAL NUMBER OF UNITS: 197
SITE ACREAGE: 19.8 AC. (862,488 SQ.FT.)
DENSITY: 10.0 DWELLING UNITS/ACRE

BUILDING/UNIT MIX:

BUILDING TYPE	NO. OF BUILDINGS	NO. OF UNITS	PLAN 1	2	3
100 (3,3)	18	36			36
200 (2,1,2)	13	39	13	26	
300 (3,2,1,2)	18	72	18	36	18
400 (1,1,1,2,3)	10	50	30	10	10
TOTAL 59		TOTAL 197	61	72	64
		PERCENTAGE OF MIX	31%	36.5%	32.5%

LEGEND:

BUILDING 100   BUILDING 200

BUILDING 300   BUILDING 400

Laurelmont, Mission Viejo, CA
Architect: Richardson Nagy Martin, Newport Beach, CA
Client: Mission Viejo Company

Townhouse configurations: Staggered units designed around auto courts

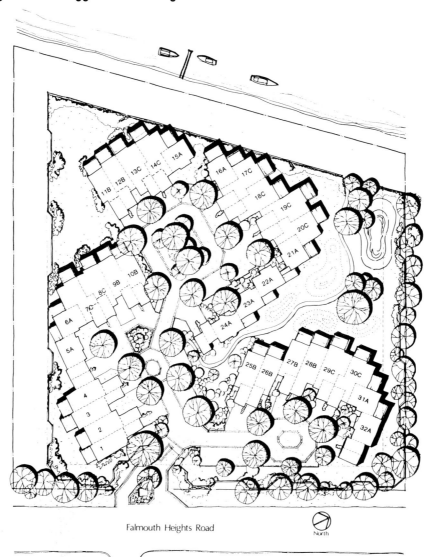

Falmouth Heights Road

North

The Boatyard, Falmouth, MA
Bloodgood Architects, P.C., Des Moines, IA
Land Planner: Matarazzo Design, Concord, NH

Townhouse configurations: Back-to-back (eight-plex)

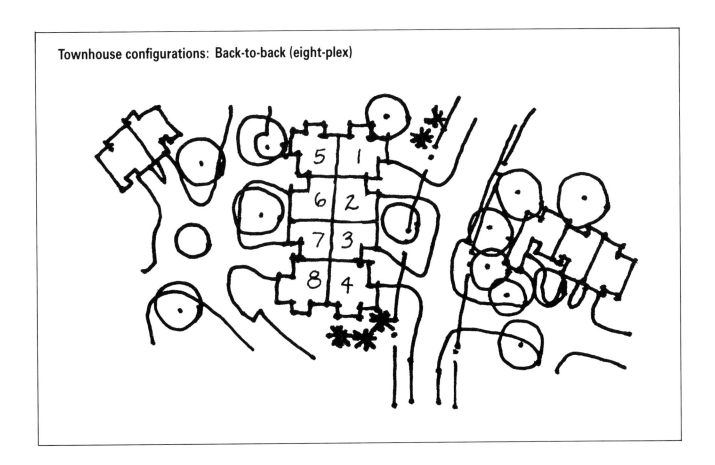

Garden Apartments/Stacked Flats

In the 1950s and 60s the term "garden apartment" signaled undesirable housing. Moratoria to halt garden apartment construction were based on the notion that garden apartment units did not contribute enough in taxes to offset the demand they generated on schools and other public services.

Recent studies have shown that notion to be unjustifiable. Many well-paid young professionals, often without children, are choosing an apartment lifestyle. This demographic group tends to stimulate the local economy rather than drain it. Moreover, the dramatic increase in condominium apartment ownership has brought a new respectability to the garden apartment. Not only are these units attractive financially, but they sport a new design treatment and an appealing new name: stacked flats.

Stacked flats feature a somewhat less rigid design approach than that found in conventional garden apartment communities, with respect to parking, common entry points, and the siting of units (Figure 37). The stacked flat provides a common entrance corridor, either open or enclosed, which allows the designer to slope or stack units in hilltown fashion on sites with no topographic variation. Parking can be provided along conventional public streets or under the building structure. The density range for stacked flats can be 30 units per acre or higher.

The design criteria that apply to 20-per-acre townhouse communities also hold for stacked flats. Trash collection and storage, vehicular access, open space, and landscaping become increasingly important as densities rise. These problems are not insurmountable; they must simply be addressed throughout the design process.

Figure 37. Stacked flat configurations

Cedar Pointe Condominiums, Denver, CO
Kaufman Meeks, Inc., Houston, TX

Concord Hill, Bellevue, WA
Architect: Mithun Bowman Emrich
Group, Bellevue, WA
Developer: Conner Development

Stacked flat configurations

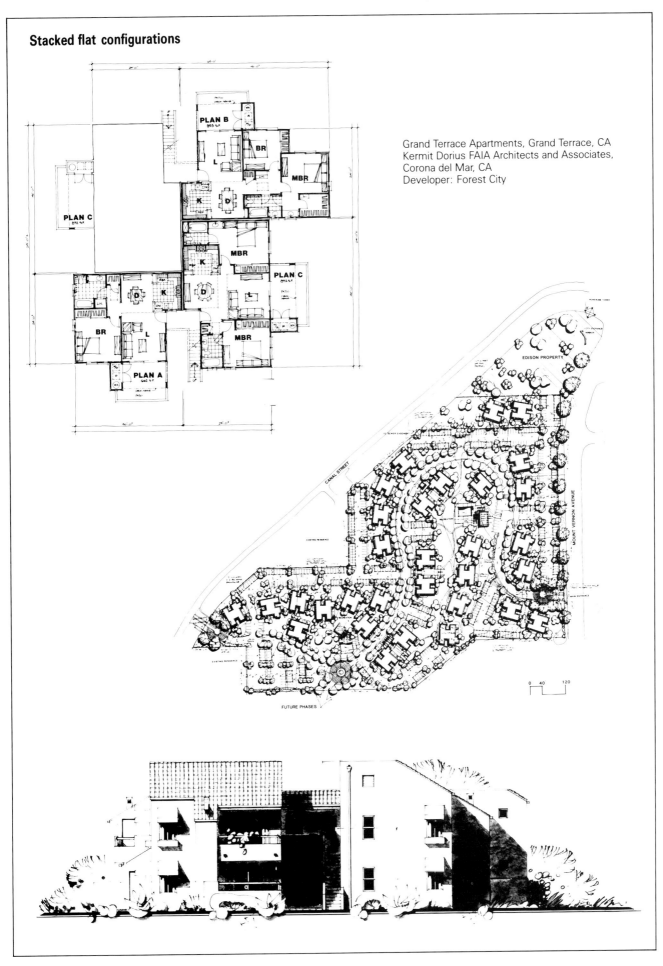

Grand Terrace Apartments, Grand Terrace, CA
Kermit Dorius FAIA Architects and Associates,
Corona del Mar, CA
Developer: Forest City

Figure 38. Roof lines, entrance treatment, and a variety of unit types enhance higher density design

The Greenhouse Condominiums, Cincinnati, OH
PDT + Co. Architects/Planners, Cincinnati, OH

Kaufman Meeks, Inc., Houston, TX

The Gables, Newton, MA
Architect: Bloodgood Architects, P.C., Des Moines, IA
Land Planner: Matarazzo Design, Concord, NH

Builder: The Green Company
Photography: Lisanti

4. Exterior Design Considerations

A number of common design elements can be identified throughout the wide range of successful higher density housing projects. These elements help attract home buyers to the lifestyle opportunities of the community, the project, and the individual unit. The project theme, established prior to the design stage, should guide every design decision made on the project—from the type of interior fixtures used to the naming of streets, to the coloring on the signage.

Exterior design is an important piece of the design puzzle. As densities increase, the opportunity for creating visually exciting building exteriors increases dramatically. The combination of roof lines, windows, entrances, and different unit types offers designers a wide range of options to create a particular lifestyle perception (Figure 38).

Building forms and details in higher density projects interact to a much greater degree than in conventional single-family housing. In a traditional single-family home, design features are less concentrated; residents may perceive only one entrance, one garage, and one set of windows at a time (Figure 39). In higher density housing, residents see not one, but four or six or ten entrances, garages, and windows in a single view. The design team must perceive this concentration of features as a buyer would: is it visually exciting or confusing? All of these details must be integrated to reinforce the theme of the project, thereby selling the buyer on the unique living environment only a higher density community can offer.

Most surveys indicate that buyers prefer a traditional single-family house with substantial square footage. Consumer preferences, however, often do not reflect today's economic realities or an understanding of desirable housing alternatives. As a result, prospective home buyers tend to evaluate higher density developments against the "traditional" single-family subdivision. By drawing on certain design elements from traditional single-family housing, builder/developers can combine the best of both worlds: affordability and the features buyers recognize as important to maintaining their lifestyle.

Some communities legislate specific design solutions, often without a complete understanding of the design options available. While community cooperation is essential to a project's success, it is more efficient for all involved to give builder/developers flexibility in doing what they do best: meeting the housing needs of the community.

Following is a discussion of exterior design considerations that are especially important to higher density home buyers. These include the need for a sense of identity, privacy, and the desire to live in a safe, attractive neighborhood.

Identity

It is essential to provide a sense of identity for each unit, particularly in attached-home projects. Chimneys, setbacks, and pushouts separate units visually. Limiting the number of attached units per building to between 4 and 6 (depending on unit size) can also reduce building mass and break up a long, repetitious facade. When doubling the number of attached units by developing stacked flats, overall design guidelines should still be observed. The scale of the building should make the buyer feel comfortable, not intimidated. In a two-story townhouse development, a one-story unit on the end of each townhouse row helps the overall building scale imitate traditional housing forms (Figure 40). Varied building heights and steep-pitched roofs provide additional unit identity and convey a single-family appearance while reducing overall scale (Figure 41).

In addition to providing each unit with a sense of identity, the designer should take care to distin-

Figure 39. Design elements are less concentrated in the conventional single-family detached house

Figure 40. Townhouses with one-story end units offer a more human building scale

Concord Hill, Bellevue, WA
Architect: Mithun Bowman Emrich Group,
Bellevue, WA
Developer: Conner Development
Photography: Gary Vannest Photography

Bel Air Condominium, Riverside, CA
Danielian Associates Architects/Planners,
Newport Beach, CA
Client: Regional Properties

guish individual entrances from the overall plane of the building. This enables the homeowner to identify a particular entry as *my front door.* Individuality can be achieved by tucking doorways back into the building with overhangs brought down to human scale. Arches, gateways, entry courts, and steep-pitched roof forms used as overhangs can also foster a sense of arrival (Figure 42).

The principles that apply to "individualizing" attached units also apply to detached units developed at higher densities. When detached homes are developed at 8 or more units per acre, they often appear as a continuous, monotonous run of units with little open space. Variations in building heights and shapes help to delineate individual homes, transforming the view from the street into an inviting picture of the community. A mix of product types—each with its own window, front porch, entrance, fireplace, and garage treatment—contribute to the project's overall attractiveness (Figure 43).

Privacy

In designing a unit (whether attached or detached) for individuality and entrance recognition, each unit should be provided with as much privacy as possible. Privacy is a traditional single-family value, and homeowners do not want to share the knowledge of their comings and goings with neighbors.

To maximize privacy, an end unit may be sited so that its entry faces a side yard. Similarly, entries of attached units should be well separated. The separation of doorways by a half flight of exterior steps, especially when covered by a distinctive overhang, can provide entry privacy. Private entrance courtyards, doorways turned away from neighboring units, and effective use of plant materials also ensure privacy while simultaneously highlighting the entrance (Figure 44).

Figure 41. Townhouses with varied heights and roof lines convey individual unit identity

Lockwood Townhomes, Bellevue, WA
Architect: Mithun Bowman Emrich Group, Bellevue, WA
Photography: Art Hupy

Windstream II, Denver, CO
Danielian Associates, Newport Beach, CA

Figure 42. Use entrances to create a sense of ownership and arrival

The Boatyard, Falmouth, MA
Bloodgood Architects, P.C., Des Moines, IA
Land Planner: Matarazzo Design, Concord, NH
Photography: Phokion Karas

Beacon Hill Vistas, Laguna Niguel, CA
Danielian Associates Architects/Planners, Newport Beach, CA

Lockwood Townhomes, Bellevue, WA
Architect: Mithun Bowman Emrich Group, Bellevue, WA
Developer: Swanson-Dean Corp.
Photography: Art Hupy

Figure 43. Higher density detached homes retain identity through individualized design treatments

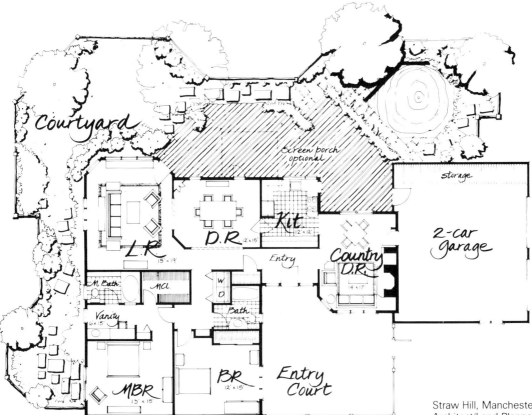

Courtyard

Screen porch optional

storage

2-car garage

Kit 12'x12'

L.R 15'x19'

D.R 12'x15'

Country D.R. 14'x17'

Entry

M.Bath

MCL

W D

Bath

Vanity 6'x15'

MBR 15'x15'

BR 12'x15'

Entry Court

Straw Hill, Manchester, NH
Architect/Land Planner: Matarazzo
Design, Concord, NH
Client: Brownfields Partnership

Summerwind, Corona del Mar, CA
Kermit Dorius FAIA Architects and Associates, Corona del Mar, CA
Client: Gfeller

Figure 44. Stairs, overhangs, entrance courtyards, and plant materials foster privacy

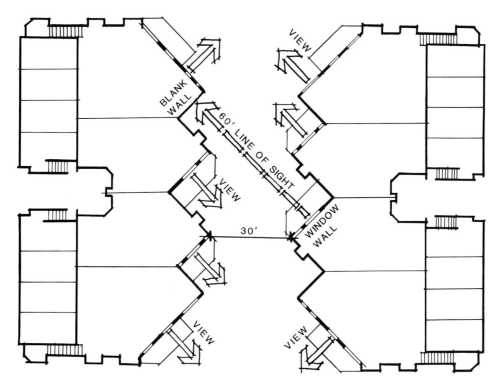

ANGLED REAR ELEVATION IS DESIGNED TO INCREASE PRIVACY BY:
1. MINIMIZING DIRECT WINDOW TO WINDOW RELATIONSHIPS.
2. MAXIMIZING VISUAL SIGHT LINES.

Bayridge, Newport Beach, CA
Architect: Richardson Nagy Martin, Newport Beach, CA
Client: J.M. Peters Company

Wonderland Hill, Boulder, CO
Downing/Leach, Boulder, CO

Pentridge Cove, Costa Mesa, CA
Danielian Associates Architects/Planners, Newport Beach, CA
Photography: David Ross

Design Consistency

As densities increase, the interaction among buildings on the site becomes especially important. To ensure a visually exciting community, buildings or units should be arranged to take advantage of site features and should offer a variety of views from the street.

In using varied roof planes, building setbacks, and building forms to achieve unit and entry individuality and privacy, remember that design elements should be consistent with the theme of the project. Individual features such as windows, overhangs, planters, trim, and chimneys should be carefully integrated into the overall project design. The use of relatively simple geometric building forms, accented with simple trim and the sensible use of one or two building materials or colors, is generally a successful design treatment (Figure 45). The strength of the design is reflected in the building's overall impact on the viewer. Too much attention to small details can distract rather than enhance the viewer's perception of the project.

Building Materials

A major selling point of any higher density community is the quality of the overall project design. The finish materials used on the exterior should relate to both local market tastes and the project theme. For example, four-inch horizontal wood siding and six-inch corner trim is popular for the ''New England'' look, just as stucco walls and tile roofs are appropriate for the ''Southwest'' style (Figure 46). Exterior materials should highlight building forms and unit identity rather than the texture of individual walls.

Exterior finishes are an important gauge of a project's perceived quality. In an area of existing neighborhoods, the sensible use of quality materials can demonstrate to concerned neighbors that the project will enhance rather than detract from the overall value and character of the area.

Building materials should be kept simple. Where there are numerous surfaces—as is the case with higher density housing—too many different materials can produce visual confusion, thereby reducing a project's overal impact and attractiveness. Careful material selection helps to integrate individual wall surfaces, permitting the viewer to perceive the project and its spaces as a single, unified environment. Exterior building surfaces thus become a subtle backdrop for the interplay of building forms and open spaces.

If carefully selected, a mix of material types can emphasize the drama of building design and can provide visual excitement. Local market preferences usually dictate the range of acceptable material styles and types. When mixing materials, consider balance, repetition, and consistency of theme. To avoid a ''busy'' look, do not use a different material for each unit within a single attached building. In some instances, it is best not to mix materials at all. The use of a single tasteful, consistent material can downplay the negative visual impact of such features as attached parking structures and fences around trashcans.

Color

Color selection for higher density development should follow general project guidelines for simplicity and consistency. Local market preferences for color should not be underestimated. Where existing single-family neighborhoods have been identified as possible sites for higher density development, the successful marketing of a new project frequently requires the use of subtle colors. The project should blend into the surrounding area—not stand out.

Color and building materials should complement one another. It is generally preferable to use different shades of the same color rather than mixing several different colors. The use of varied shades of brown in siding, brick, and wood trim, for example, helps achieve a consistent ''earthy'' look.

Color can be used to highlight specific features of building design such as hardware, balconies, railings, and roof shapes. Adding color to these elements reinforces their shape, providing visual excitement and individual identity to higher density units. Color can also be introduced in the nonresidential aspects of the development, such as signage, fences, and landscaping, as long as it is consistent with the overall project theme.

While it is becoming increasingly popular to use colors not typically associated with residential development, caution in color selection is advised. Since color is highly market-sensitive, it should be used to reinforce theme and should appeal to the market segment toward which the development is geared. New color shades used for the sake of fad or innovation should be avoided. Only those colors that contribute to the design message of the project should be used.

Solar Access

Although solar planning for residential buildings requires more coverage than this book allows, it is important to consider the impact of sunlight patterns on individual units—whether or not they are designed for reliance on solar energy.

Homeowners enjoy sunlight in their homes. Therefore, when designing higher density housing, it is important that all units have access to sunlight. With the trend toward smaller-than-traditional homes, maximum natural light makes units feel larger and more vibrant.

When units are built close together, consider the shading patterns of individual buildings on adjacent

Figure 45. Use simple building forms and materials for higher density development

Lockwood Townhomes, Bellevue, WA
Architect: Mithun Bowman Emrich Group, Bellevue, WA
Developer: Swanson-Dean Corp.
Photography: Art Hupy

Windstream II, Denver, CO
Danielian Associates Architects/Planners, Newport Beach, CA

buildings, parking areas, open spaces, and sidewalks. Buildings should not permanently shade other buildings. Similarly, spaces between buildings should receive some sunlight every day.

In cold weather climates, sidewalks and parking areas should be exposed to as much sunlight as possible. Open spaces and unit entries, which are important design elements in higher density projects, should also be highlighted with sunlight. If these spaces are permanently shaded, or are covered in ice or snow throughout the winter, they will have a negative impact on the community. A sunny, open entry sequence to a building unit is a valuable asset in the perception of "arrival."

Similarly, hot and sunny climates will require the use of baffles or other shading mechanisms to control sunlight access. The use of controlled shade can reduce or control excessive heat buildup and provide welcome relief (Figure 47).

Landscape Plan/Site Furniture

The landscape plan plays an important role in higher density development—both within the project itself and in the surrounding community. The land-

scape architect becomes a valuable member of the design team by tying plant material selections to the theme of the project, its site and surroundings.

As densities increase, yard areas decrease and become more critical to the overall design. In higher density projects, each design detail is important in helping to sell the product. The side and rear yards of zero lot line houses, for example, should be designed as an extension of the inside space (Figure 48). The selection and grouping of plant material is important in achieving that transition. Likewise, air conditioning units, gas and electric meters, trash storage areas and the like are more visible in higher density designs. Using plants or compatible building materials to screen and soften the effect of these necessary fixtures can be very effective (Figure 49).

A project's image is established by the effectiveness of its landscape treatment. Entrances to the development and to individual units can be enhanced by the creative use of plant materials (Figure 50). The entrance can be clearly identified so that each buyer feels that he/she has arrived *home.* Similarly, plantings can be used to blend with or screen from adjacent uses. This can include preservation of existing tree masses, supplementing what exists

Figure 46. Use exterior building materials to appeal to local market preferences and convey overall project theme

Rawlins Street Condominiums, Dallas, TX
Womack/Humphreys Architects, Dallas, TX
Client: Anderson Association

Turtle Rock Pointe, Irvine, CA
Architect: Richardson Nagy Martin, Newport Beach, CA
Client: J.M. Peters Company

Somerset Wharf, Savannah, GA
Architect: Richardson Nagy Martin, Newport Beach, CA
Client: Colonial Properties

with new specimens, and planting wildflowers in common open areas such as storm drainage ways. The builder/developer should use plant materials that are indigenous to the site to enhance the project. Work distinctive local features, whether manmade or natural, into the landscape plan and unit design (Figure 51).

The builder/developer should not be afraid of using berms in flat areas or flat areas in hilly sections, placing plant groupings in clear areas, or using other landscape design elements to enhance the overall project image.

Site furniture is another higher density design element that requires careful attention to detail. Site furniture can include:

- Lighting fixtures
- Street signs and other signage
- Benches
- Fences and walls
- Trash receptacles
- Mailboxes

It is the landscape architect's responsibility to blend these elements with the overall project theme to convey a sense of *arrival, home,* and *neighborhood.* A community whose theme is country charm, for example, might feature white picket fences and ''gaslight'' lampposts (Figure 52). A cosmopolitan European theme, on the other hand, might be carried out through ornate wrought iron benches, lighting fixtures, fences, trash receptacles, and the like.

Figure 47. Use exterior shading mechanisms to control sunlight access

Park Centre, Mesa, AZ
Danielian Associates Architects/Planners, Newport Beach, CA
Photography: John Bare & Associates

The Gables, Newton Center, MA
Bloodgood Architects, P.C., Des Moines, IA
Land Planner: Matarazzo Design, Concord, NH
Client: The Green Company, Inc.
Photography: Phokion Karas

Figure 48. Yard areas extend interior living space of higher density homes

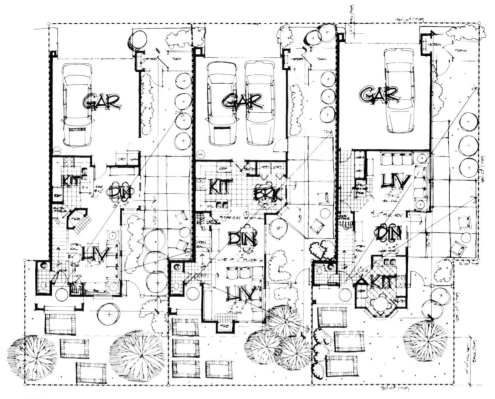

EDI Architects/Planners, Houston, TX

Turtle Rock Pointe, Irvine, CA
Architect: Richardson Nagy Martin,
Newport Beach, CA
Client: J.M. Peters Company

Figure 49. Use plants or compatible building materials to mask utility and other fixtures

Wonderland Hill, Boulder, CO
Downing/Leach, Boulder, CO

Figure 50. Use plant materials to enhance entrances to the development and to individual units

Wonderland Hill, Boulder, CO
Downing/Leach, Boulder, CO

The Boatyard, Falmouth, MA
Bloodgood Architects, P.C., Des Moines, IA
Land Planner: Matarazzo Design,
Concord, NH
Photography: Phokion Karas

Foxgate, Culver City, CA
Danielian Associates Architects/Planners, Newport Beach, CA
Photography: The Lee Side, Inc.

Figure 51. Incorporate distinctive local features into unit design and the landscape plan

Cobblestone, Indianapolis, IN
Bloodgood Architects, P.C., Des Moines, IA
Photography: Gary Chilluffo

Treetops, Falmouth, MA
Architect: Miquelle Associates,
Melrose, MA
Land Planner: Matarazzo Design,
Concord, NH
Client: The Green Company

Figure 52. Site furniture expresses project theme

Concord Hill, Bellevue, WA
Architect: Mithun Bowman Emrich Group,
Bellevue, WA
Developer: Conner Development

Parking

Nothing destroys the appearance or sales appeal of a development more quickly than inadequate and unsightly parking facilities. This is particularly true in higher density designs, which tend to have high concentrations of vehicles.

Most local ordinances establish minimum parking requirements on a per-unit basis, although practical market considerations often require a different unit-to-parking ratio. In some projects, the number of spaces per unit can be decreased based on the car-owning pattern of the target market. For example, residents of a retirement community may not always require two spaces per unit, while young families may need two-and-a-half or three spaces.

Regulations governing parking were written in response to problems created by inadequate parking in projects built in the 1950s and 60s. The biases fostered by development in an earlier era can be overcome through negotiation with local government and the application of sound planning standards. Local government should grant builders flexibility in meeting the needs of potential buyers without requiring compliance with arbitrary and often inappropriate standards.

As discussed earlier, a higher density community's appearance depends upon the successful integration of design forms, details, building materials, and distinctive unit identities. The added requirement of offstreet parking can dominate an otherwise attractive streetscape. Since the most important feature of a project is its homes—not its parking facilities—the design team should downplay the impact of parking as much as possible by achieving a balance between unit design features, open space, and parking.

Parking in Detached Home Developments

In single-family detached home developments, whether zero lot line or conventional, there are a number of approaches to solving the parking problem. Visitor parking, always a homeowner concern, can be provided in the street right-of-way. Combinations of parking techniques can be used throughout a project, although long, uninterrupted rows of parking spaces or facilities should be avoided from both an aesthetic and marketing viewpoint. The creative use of grass islands with trees or earth mounds can break up parking areas and add buyer appeal to a project (Figure 53).

Where more spaces are provided per unit than the minimum required, the extra spaces should be counted toward the visitor allotment. For example, if each unit has four spaces onsite, and the requirement is two per unit, the two extra spaces should go towards reducing the number of required visitor spaces. This "crediting" system helps to eliminate excessive parking and pavement areas.

When garages are used, they can be angled or staggered to create a more pleasing and less monotonous streetscape; they can also be used in combination with well-scaled carports or shelters. Where space permits, garages can be turned ninety degrees so that the garage door faces away from the street. Combinations of front-facing and side-facing garages are another option. This technique is particularly applicable to smaller lot detached units with reduced lot frontages, which tend to suffer from design monotony. Garages can also be tucked under units to minimize street impact (Figure 54). In general, units set back twenty feet from a traditional public street can accommodate one vehicle on a concrete pad and one in the garage.

Parking in Attached Home Developments

Attached units usually present a different kind of parking problem. Most typically, cars are parked in lots or compounds designed to accommodate several vehicles. 200 feet is generally assumed to be an acceptable walking distance from unit to parking. This figure varies depending upon market demand, climate, project design, and topography. Some buyers prefer a lot or unit that is not in view of the parking lot. Other consumers require parking to be right outside their front door. Builder/developers and the design team must know the preferences of the market, and should plan accordingly.

The higher the density, the greater the impact of parking facilities on the community as a whole. For example, parking in a project of 18 to 24 units per acre can account for nearly 50 percent of the total development site. As with detached-home projects, creative techniques for accommodating the automobile should be applied (Figure 53).

Parking provided in compounds or as part of a cul-de-sac design can be screened by plant materials in combination with earth mounding and other landscaping techniques. Textured blocks can reduce the impact of paved surfaces, and help to absorb stormwater as well. It is not uncommon to find garages, carports, and tuck-under parking in high-priced attached unit projects as well as in detached-home communities. The problem facing the designer is how to manage the building mass of densely built units plus garages. Techniques include the use of plantings, variations in building material, and design variety in garages and the homes themselves. For example, an upward-sloping garage roof that faces the street is more subtle than a gable-end garage roof that dominates the streetscape.

Figure 53. Parking options in higher density development

Landscaped parking areas

Wonderland Hill, Boulder, CO
Downing/Leach, Boulder, CO

Allowances for visitor parking

Ledgewood Hills, Nashua, NH
Architect: Page Michaelis Rudolph, P.C., Nashua, NH
Land Planner: Matarazzo Design, Concord, NH
Client: H.J. Stabile and Son

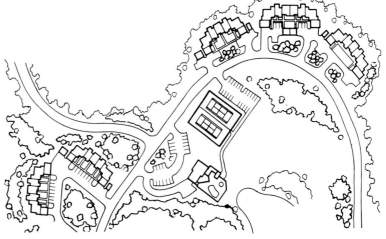

"Motor courts" integrated into a zero lot line design

EDI Architects/Planners, Houston, TX

Figure 54. Garage treatments

Rear-loaded and tucked-under garages

Concord Hill, Bellevue, WA
Architect: Mithun Bowman Emrich Group, Bellevue, WA
Developer: Conner Development

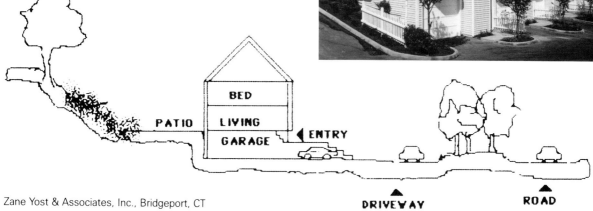

Zane Yost & Associates, Inc., Bridgeport, CT

Attached-unit garages with tucked-under parking oriented around courts

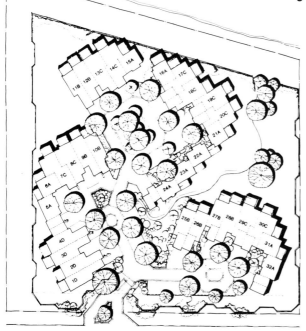

The Boatyard, Falmouth, MA
Bloodgood Architects, P.C., Des Moines, IA
Land Planner: Matarazzo Design, Concord, NH
Photography: Phokion Karas

Combination of front- and side-facing garages

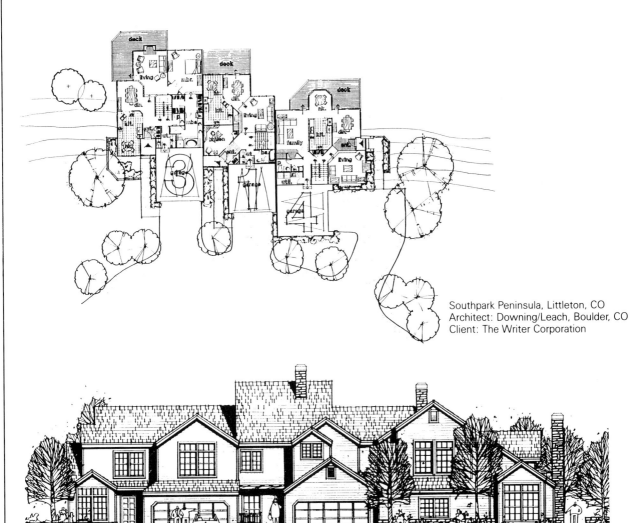

Southpark Peninsula, Littleton, CO
Architect: Downing/Leach, Boulder, CO
Client: The Writer Corporation

Integration of garage mass with unit mass

Lockwood Townhomes, Bellevue, WA
Architect: Mithun Bowman Emrich Group,
Bellevue, WA
Developer: Swanson-Dean Corp.

Figure 55. Visual progression from confined to open space enhances the feeling of volume

Summerwind, Corona del Mar, CA
Kermit Dorius FAIA Architects and Associates, Corona del Mar, CA
Client: Gfeller
Photography: Steve Carmer

5. Interior Design Considerations

The streamlined living areas in today's higher density homes reflect consumer demands for exciting, efficient, and affordable housing. The special qualities of higher density living allow homeowners to spend more of their free time enjoying their home and less time maintaining it. Because today's buyers may be willing to sacrifice floor space for affordability does not mean, however, that they are willing to sacrifice quality.

Higher density housing must be designed to provide more quality amenities than traditional detached units. To create buyer excitement, the project team must understand what types of features trigger the decision of particular markets to buy. Monthly trade publications are one good resource for staying current on today's consumer preferences. These ideas can be adapted by a good designer to suit the local market.

Volume

Creative use of volume achieves a sense of spaciousness and excitement in higher density homes. Individual units can be designed to feel large and bright by opening up rooms and circulation space, capitalizing on light and views, and exploiting the spatial dimensions of length, width, and especially height. Volume can work in all areas of the unit. Living and sleeping areas, kitchens, and baths all gain by the use of volume space.

Buyers have learned to appreciate the volume of a space as opposed to merely square footage. The key is to extend the distance perceived by the eye in a single view. Remember, however, that the effective use of volume requires a visible progression of ceiling heights. It is the change from a confined space to an open space that creates the dramatic effect (Figure 55). For example, progression from an 8-foot-high foyer into a living room with a 16-foot vaulted ceiling makes the second space seem much larger than its actual area dimensions.

Changes in volume can be accomplished in a number of ways. One- or two-level stepdowns and stepups are conventional ways to achieve height changes. The use of a full or partial scissors truss allows the ceiling to slope upward while providing space for attic insulation. Simple increases in room heights also work. The cost of heating and cooling additional volume space is usually offset by the reduced amount of wall surface exposed to the exterior.

Depending on local market preferences, smaller units can be made to feel more spacious by combining separate, smaller rooms into larger multipurpose areas. This increases the distance seen by the eye, making the unit seem larger. Careful furniture arrangements, differences in floor surfaces, and changes in ceiling height can separate activity areas in a house without the use of walls.

The use of shared space can be especially effective in two different activity areas of the house: living and sleeping. The "great room," a room type that has become popular in recent years, includes the dining area and a combination formal living/informal family room space. When the kitchen opens onto the great room, the entire space functions as a high impact, major activity area (Figure 56).

Another area that benefits from openness is the master bedroom. Most market surveys indicate that the master bedroom/bath space is an important factor in home purchase decisions. By eliminating unnecessary doors, increasing closet space, and expanding the size of the master bath slightly, an otherwise small bedroom can become a spacious master suite (Figure 57). Openness in this area, especially when accentuated with a vaulted ceiling, can substantially increase the market value of the master suite.

Light

The use of light and views in individual units helps to make smaller plans seem more spacious and visually appealing. In higher density projects, energy requirements and limited exterior wall area may reduce the number of windows per unit. The careful placement of windows can strengthen the relationship between exterior and interior, extending the perceived spaciousness of the unit. Windows should take advantage of available vistas, with views for each unit coordinated during the planning stage to ensure that the living room of one unit does not face into an adjacent unit's bedroom.

Figure 56. The "great room" combines dining area with formal/informal living space to create a major activity center

Landmark at Indian Creek, Denver, CO
Bloodgood Architects, P.C., Des Moines, IA
Builder: Brock Homes/Denver
Photography: G. Van Cleave

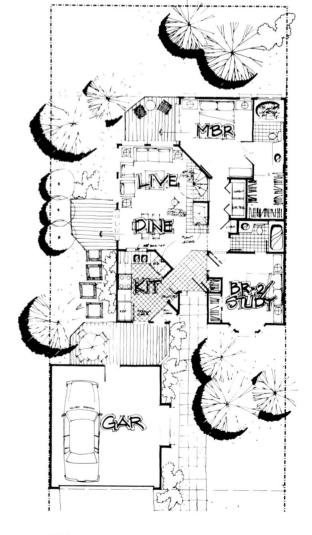

EDI Architects/Planners, Houston, TX

Figure 57. Master suite features expanded closet and bath areas

Sun Lakes, Indianapolis, IN
Bloodgood Architects, P.C., Des Moines, IA
Builder: Hansen & Horn
Photography: Hedrich Blessing

To make the most effective use of light and space, windows may be placed together at corners. This creates a broad vista that draws the eye outdoors and downplays the small scale of the unit. At the same time, wall space is freed up for flexible furniture placement (Figure 58).

Skylights are also popular features for introducing light into smaller spaces. They expand the feeling of space by creating a focal point and drawing the eye outward to the view beyond. Skylights introduce natural light into windowless spaces such as lofts, bathrooms, and kitchens, turning confined areas into appealing and marketable features. The addition of skylights to spaces that traditionally use artificial light also increases dramatic effect.

Exterior Views and Privacy

Using exterior areas to expand interior space helps to incorporate each unit and its yard into a project's overall environment and lifestyle. The extent to which interior and exterior are integrated depends on climate and local market preferences. When the views within the unit are directed outside, the exterior areas should be developed as an extension of the living space, reinforcing the sense of private ownership (Figure 59). The layout of decks, gardens, and patios should correspond with appropriate interior activity areas; sliding glass doors may be used for access.

Outdoor living areas should be planned for privacy. The relationship between a unit's exterior spaces, its interior, and adjacent homes must be considered. Full-height fences that define private spaces are acceptable if they fit into the project's overall design. Other design treatments that ensure privacy include the separation of entrances, the orientation of units in different directions, and the arrangement of views toward open spaces.

Privacy considerations are essential to interior planning as well. Attached higher density development is characterized by shared walls. The design team must plan for the activities that occur on both sides of the wall. Spaces designed for similar activities should be sited adjacent to each other so that one unit's bedroom does not share a wall with the next unit's living room. Interior stairwells should be located against a wall to provide sound insulation between attached units. Closets can also be used as

Figure 58. Corner windows make effective use of light and space

Sun Lakes, Indianapolis, IN
Bloodgood Architects, P.C., Des Moines, IA
Builder: Hansen & Horn
Photography: Hedrich Blessing

Figure 59. Use exterior views to extend interior space perception

Preston Village, Dallas, TX
Womack/Humphreys Architects, Dallas, TX
Client: Sanford Homes

Figure 60. Opening the kitchen to adjacent rooms creates a lighter, airier effect

Straw Hill, Manchester, NH
Architect/Land Planner: Matarazzo Design,
Concord, NH
Client: Brownfields Partnership
Photography: Paul Avis

Figure 61. Bathrooms can communicate spaciousness and luxury in a higher density home

Willowcreek at River Run, Boise, ID
Downing/Leach, Boulder, CO

buffers. In back-to-back unit arrangements, plumbing trees for kitchens and baths can be backed up to simplify plumbing layouts and keep water-related sounds within the same general area in each unit.

Kitchens and Baths

Kitchens and baths should receive special attention, because these two areas are of vital interest to home buyers. The impact of these rooms adds more to the perception of the unit than any other area, with the possible exception of the unit's entrance.

Kitchens in downsized units are often small, reflecting smaller household size and a lifestyle that usually does not include elaborate meal preparation and formal entertaining. Nonetheless, kitchens need to feel spacious and should be opened to the rest of the living area. Pass-throughs, eating counters, and work islands define the kitchen and provide efficiency without interrupting the flow of space. Opening a kitchen allows it to steal light from windows in adjacent rooms and command greater attention within the home. Shutters or elevated countertops can be used to hide work areas. Luxury features such as ceramic tile, quality cabinetry, and greenhouse windows assume greater importance when viewed from other areas of the house. The kitchen can become a positive focus of the living area, depending on market tastes (Figure 60). The NAHB publication, *Kitchens,* provides additional information on designing this important room.

The bath is another room that can communicate spaciousness and luxury effectively (Figure 61). Today's minimum standard bathroom size is five feet by seven. Any increase is considered a luxury, particularly in a downsized house. Since consumers perceive increased square footage in the bathroom more readily than they notice a decrease in bedroom size, a tradeoff can be made. Compartmentalizing the bath can also make it function better. In the master bedroom, entering the bathroom through a walk-in closet creates a spacious dressing suite. An increase in the size of bathroom mirrors to full vertical height enhances the perception of both height and depth. Skylights are also effective, as noted above.

6. Public Service Provisions

With cutbacks in federal funds, local governments are seeking ways to provide basic services more efficiently and cost-effectively. Higher density development offers opportunities for lowering public service costs and increasing housing affordability. When units are located close together on small lots, or are attached in clusters, such elements as street layout and public service and utility delivery can be designed for maximum cost-effectiveness.

Street Design

Street design is an essential element of higher density development. Construction costs for residential streets account for the second largest percentage of total lot development costs. Only the land cost itself is higher (Figure 62).

Traditional local codes typically specify two or three basic residential street design alternatives that must be used in project planning. The rights-of-way and paving widths established in these codes are set without considering the actual use and traffic volume of a given street. Standards are set on a community-wide basis, regardless of market conditions, design considerations, or site characteristics.

For example, many communities require the developer to use the same standard whether constructing a street to serve ten units or several hundred units. Yet residential streets have a wide range of needs and functions. A hierarchy of street types is called for, based upon projected use. Figure 63 shows the function of each street type and the average daily traffic count for each. Street systems based upon these criteria meet actual needs rather than arbitrary standards.

Access

Concern over vehicular access—private, service, and emergency—is one of the most common problems in establishing street standards for higher density developments. Access for service and emergency vehicles is especially critical in the eyes of public officials. Local public works engineers generally maintain that adequate access requires wide street pavements and rights-of-way. Yet access can be provided without wasteful use of land for wide

streets. Arranging attached and detached units around courts or in cul-de-sacs reduces the length of street that vehicles must travel to reach their destination (Figure 64). Good higher density development makes use of these techniques on a project-wide basis to reduce the total amount of street construction. These reductions result in a lower house price for the consumer and reduced maintenance costs for the community.

It is interesting to note the origins of the wide street pavement requirements. In mid-19th century Salt Lake City, Utah, Brigham Young needed 100-foot-wide streets to turn around his mule teams. Those street standards are still in use today. Similarly, cul-de-sac size evolved from a time when fire trucks did not have a reverse gear and required a large turning radius. Modern fire equipment, like modern housing, has been downsized and streamlined; however, local street standards often have not changed with the times.

The intent of local regulations is to permit all emergency vehicles to exit from a court or cul-de-sac without turning around after responding to an emergency. Studies demonstrate, however, that in an actual emergency no vehicle can exit easily from a cul-de-sac or any residential street regardless of pavement width. In the case of a fire, for example, fire trucks, the fire chief's car, ambulances, police cars, and neighborhood residents' vehicles all block easy egress. Most vehicles must either back out of the street or turn around in a driveway, even on excessively wide streets and cul-de-sacs. The point to remember is that pavement width alone does not guarantee good access. Street widths should be based on actual traffic requirements and adequate access provisions rather than traditional width-based standards.

How can emergency and service vehicle access be achieved without wide streets? In higher density designs, open space for the common use of residents provides one alternative to direct access via a public street. Pedestrian paths designed to form a wheel track have also been successful. Likewise, steel or masonry grids placed under a grass surface provide a firm surface for emergency vehicles. Yet another option is to construct movable bollards which allow

Figure 62. Land Development Cost Summary

Source: *The Affordable Housing Demonstration, Phoenix, Arizona—A Case Study*
U.S. Department of Housing and Urban Development

Activity	As Built	Existing Standards	Savings
Raw land	$1,254,000	$1,254,000	$ —
Vertical curbs	31,212	50,039	18,827
Roll curbs/sidewalks	53,065	71,544	18,479
Curb return radius	18,363	26,808	8,445
Streets	183,240	219,585	36,345
Stormwater drainage	36,853	107,431	70,578
Water service	109,162	112,325	3,163
Sanitary sewer	112,208	171,879	59,671
Electrical service	24,541	35,168	10,627
Driveway entrances	11,978	24,661	12,683
Landscaping, irrigation	159,828	168,452	8,624
Totals	$1,994,450	$2,241,892	$247,442
Cost Per Unit	$7,821*	$11,497**	$3,676

*255 units as built
**195 units if built to existing standards

Figure 63. Hierarchy of street types

- COLLECTORS: CONDUCT TRAFFIC BETWEEN MAJOR ARTERIALS AND/OR ACTIVITY CENTERS...28'-36'
- SUBCOLLECTOR: TYPICAL RESIDENTIAL STREET ....24'-26'
- PLACE OR LANE: CUL-DE-SACS UP TO 300' IN LENGTH................20'-22'

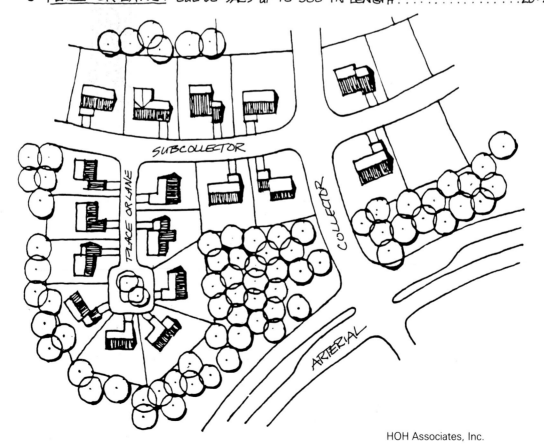

HOH Associates, Inc.

Figure 64. Arranging units around courts or cul-de-sacs reduces overall street length

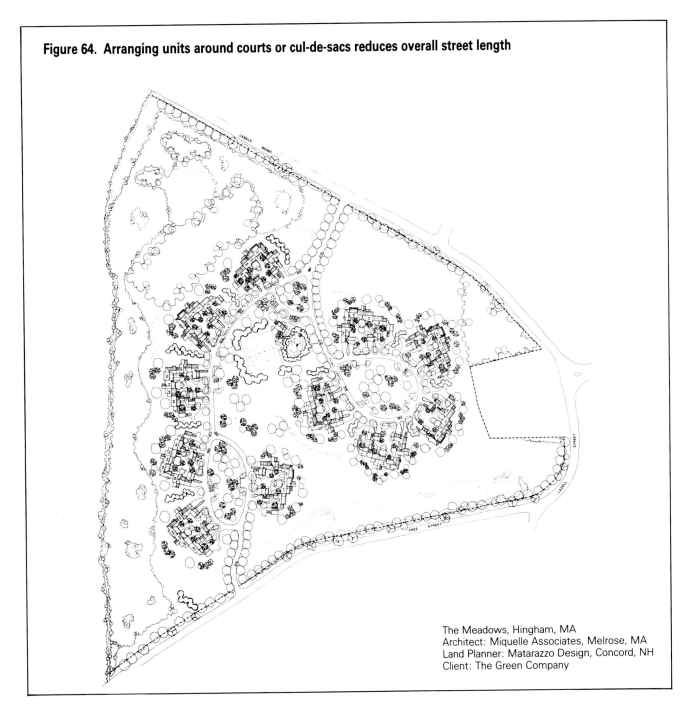

The Meadows, Hingham, MA
Architect: Miquelle Associates, Melrose, MA
Land Planner: Matarazzo Design, Concord, NH
Client: The Green Company

emergency vehicles to drive on sidewalks or other paved areas that are usually off limits to vehicles.

Many local regulations permit narrower streets, but only if they are to be privately maintained. Frequently these private streets must be constructed to public standards but without the accompanying right-of-way. If private streets are adequate to protect the health, safety, and welfare of residents as required by the local zoning code, then their maintenance should be a public responsibility.

Many builders and developers have successfully reduced street widths through communication and negotiation with local fire chiefs and public works engineers. Seminars can also be used to outline the benefits of using a variety of streets to serve specific needs. In some communities, the building industry and local government have developed a continuing mechanism for monitoring street performance to keep their standards current.

Cul-de-sacs

As mentioned above, cul-de-sacs are an attractive, cost-effective street design alternative for higher density communities. Land planners have come up with a variety of approaches to cul-de-sac design. Among the more common are Y-shape, T-shape, and squares or circles with interior parking (Figure 65). Because of concerns about public service delivery—emergency access, trash removal, and so on—local development codes often prohibit these designs. Yet the new designs generally provide the same or better service levels in a more manageable, cost-effective, and aesthetically pleasing manner than conventional street configurations.

Cul-de-sacs have other advantages as well. First, the reduction in paving helps to address the problem of stormwater runoff by limiting the amount of impervious surface. The stormwater infiltration, when used with grass swales, helps to replenish the groundwater supply and to reduce problems of downstream flooding. Variety in cul-de-sac design can also allow for the preservation of existing trees within cul-de-sac islands. Frequently, local codes dictate the removal of trees because of dimensional specifications for lots and roads.

Figure 65. Cul-de-sac design options

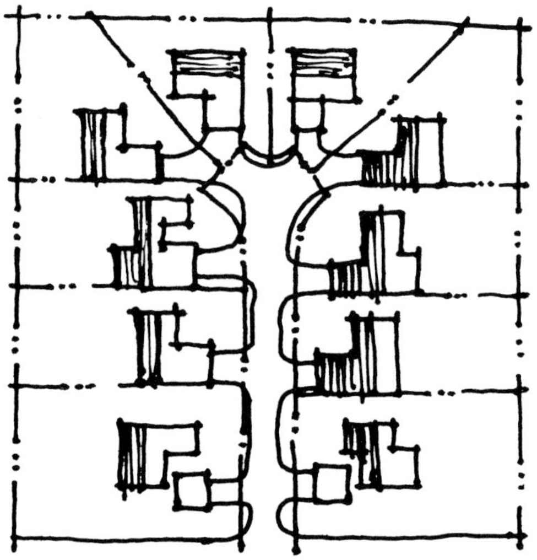

Y-shape
Michael F. Shibley

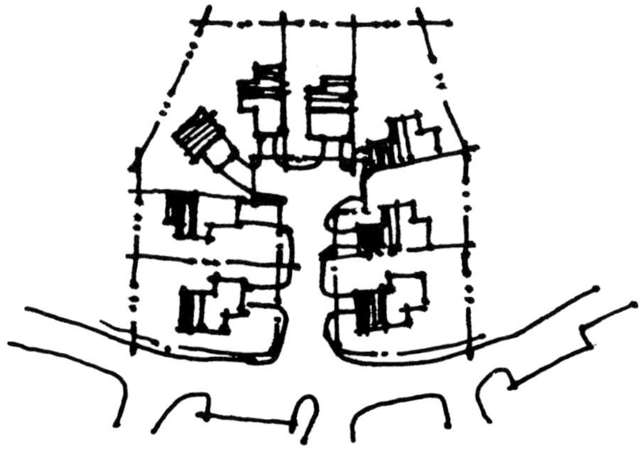

T-shape
Michael F. Shibley

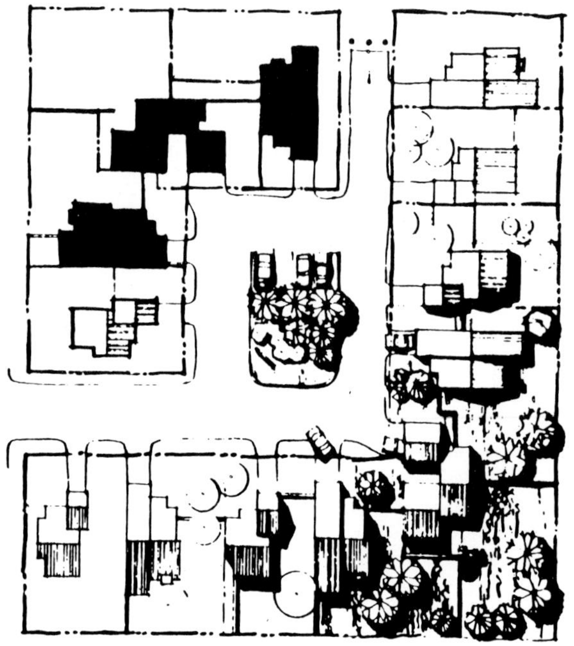

Square with interior parking
David Jensen Associates, Inc., Denver, CO

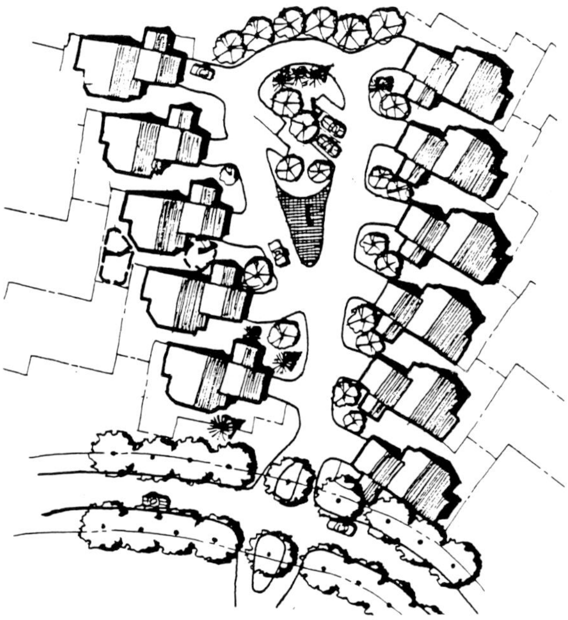

Circle variation with interior parking
David Jensen Associates, Inc., Denver, CO

Service Delivery

As land planners and builder/developers seek creative approaches to more affordable housing, public service providers must rethink service delivery methods. Localities should not turn down higher density development because trash collectors and meter readers object to performing their jobs in a non-traditional manner; rather, creative approaches to providing these services should be explored. For example, trash collection points can be designated at the entrances to short cul-de-sacs, or service alleys can be incorporated into the design. Some jurisdictions would have to amend their codes, however, to eliminate the prohibition against alleys.

Electric Meters

Electric meters in conventional, low density single-family developments are generally installed on a house-by-house basis. With the emergence of zero lot line detached units and a wide variety of attached units, however, it has become necessary to locate meters at the rear of units or in clusters at a convenient, visible location. The aesthetic appearance of many projects has been degraded by utility company policies that require meters to be accessible from the front of the house. Creative builders can devise ways to screen front-mounted meters or to arrange for alternative meter placement at the rear of all units, permitting the meter reader access without wasted steps. Compromises and design alternatives that serve the needs of the utility company, the buyer, and the community must be developed.

Water and Sewer

Reductions in setbacks made possible by clustering units and lots translate into lower installation costs for water and sewer systems. When houses are sited closer to service roads, driveways are shorter. This reduces the linear runs of pipe and pavement needed to serve individual units or building groups. The main service lines located in the street can also be shortened when units are clustered (Figure 66).

In unsewered development areas, clusters can be served with onsite sewage treatment facilities. Package plants are available, ranging from individual facilities for each lot to plants with a capacity for 100 homes or more.

Common Trenching

Common trenching is a technique in which all utilities—electric, gas, telephone, cable TV, and water mains—are placed in one excavated right-of-way trench. This practice eliminates much construction activity and therefore much of the energy consumed by cutting and filling. By eliminating multiple rights-of-way, much land is freed for other productive purposes (Figure 67).

It is relatively common for communities to permit the placement of cable TV, telephone and electric lines in the same trench. It is less common to find water and sewer together. The concept of common trenching is not always prohibited by local government, but rather by the utility companies. The utility companies frequently cannot agree among themselves about the placement of facilities. This lack of cooperation has prevented widespread implementation of the common trenching concept.

In one community, the local public works department strictly prohibits the use of street rights-of-way for anything other than city water and sewer lines.

Figure 67. Common utility trench

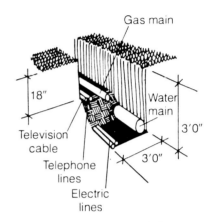

The other utility companies are left to negotiate with the developer about where their facilities will be located. It is ironic that such disagreements have arisen over use of street rights-of-way, since wide rights-of-way are generally provided for utility placement. A better organized, more cooperative system is needed for making utility location decisions.

Snow Removal

Snow removal is a regional concern, but a critical one in any snowfall area where higher density developments are found. Provisions for clearing snow from the narrower, shorter streets that serve higher density units can be made during the design process.

The land planner has several options. First, open space designated as pedestrian walkways can double as snow storage areas in the winter, when walkways are rarely used. Playgrounds, similarly unused during winter months, provide additional snow storage areas. Cul-de-sac islands offer still another opportunity for snow storage. Snowplows can drive around a cul-de-sac in a clockwise direction to avoid pushing the snow into driveways, and can deposit snow in the center island instead. High snowfall regions of the country obviously require larger storage areas. Whatever the circumstances, local regulations should allow the builder/ developer flexibility to accommodate snow removal in the most effective way for the project and site.

Figure 66. Water and sewer installation costs can be reduced in a cluster plan

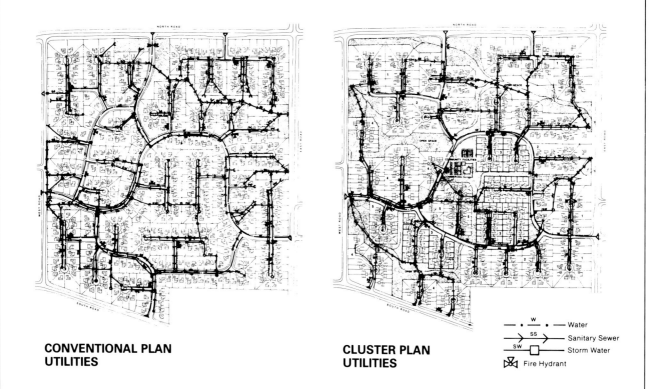

CONVENTIONAL PLAN UTILITIES

CLUSTER PLAN UTILITIES

— • — w — • — Water
→ ss → Sanitary Sewer
sw → Storm Water
⊠ Fire Hydrant

SUMMARY OF SITE DEVELOPMENT COSTS

	CONVENTIONAL		CLUSTER	
	Total Costs	Costs/DU	Total Costs	Costs/DU
Street Pavement	$ 862,165	$ 1,827	$ 540,569	$1,145
Curbs and Gutters	433,872	919	—	—
Street Trees	412,496	874	374,640	794
Driveways	743,400	1,575	527,715	1,213
Storm Drainage	696,464	1,476	278,295	590
Water Distribution	746,044	1,581	492,792	1,044
Sanitary Sewer	1,142,647	2,421	1,009,601	2,139
Grading	332,044	703	220,755	468
Clearing/Grubbing	156,915	332	109,785	233
Sidewalks	209,250	443	197,775	419
Subtotal	$5,735,298	$12,151	$3,751,927	$8,045
Engineering Fees (5.8%)	332,647	705	217,612	467
Total	**$6,067,945**	**$12,856**	**$3,969,539**	**$8,512**
Actual Difference on a per lot basis		**4,344**		
% of Conventional lot cost		100%		66%

Marketing

Marketing

Introduction

Marketing is the art—and science—of communicating a product's benefits to a target audience. The marketing of higher density housing must focus on the advantages of living in a higher density environment. The challenge to the marketer is to combine knowledge of the consumer (derived from research) with an ability to provide the products they want (a function of production and management). The task includes representing the consumer while managing the business to maintain or increase pro forma profits.

Higher density housing suffers from certain misconceptions, which an effective marketing strategy will seek to overcome. Among them:

- Higher density attached homes are another form of apartments—so why buy them?
- Detached higher density homes do not have adequate yard space.
- There is little privacy.
- There is little perceived individuality among units in a higher density community.
- There is little personalized outdoor space.

Higher density housing presents builder/developers with both a challenge and an opportunity. Market research, architecture, land planning, and engineering can be skillfully combined to create living environments that appeal to the consumer in unique ways. Some of the most innovative higher density communities have been developed in recent years in response to new political and economic trends. If builder/developers understand the remarkable changes occurring in the marketplace, they will be able to truly communicate the benefits of the higher density product.

For example, many of today's working couples don't want to be bothered with maintenance; nor do the single-headed households that are becoming more prevalent. Further, well-planned lot configurations of higher density detached product can yield more usable yard space than a traditional product on lots 25 percent larger. As higher density design and unit-to-unit privacy improve, the builder/developer can build for today's markets with confidence.

Ideally, the marketing process begins prior to property acquisition. As discussed in the Planning section, market research can dictate target markets, opportunities, and product which, in turn, define property acquisition criteria. This includes zoning, topography, neighborhood and community characteristics. Marketing is an interactive process with the builder's other disciplines, including staffing, accounting, and construction. In reality, almost every action taken by a builder has marketing implications.

The marketing plan provides a framework from which all marketing activity is directed and measured. The marketing plan includes a marketing strategy for competitive advantage and a business plan for administration, including budgets, objectives, staffing, and controls. An effective marketing plan considers the following elements:

- Research and analysis (discussed in the Planning section of this book)
- Budgets and controls
- Target markets
- Traffic goals
- Sales goals
- Product development
- Pricing, financing, and phasing
- Merchandising and presentation
- Advertising
- Promotion
- Sales
- Public relations
- Post-sale relations
- Post-sale management

These elements, as they pertain to higher density development, are addressed below.

A key issue to consider in developing and implementing a marketing plan is flexibility, because today's housing consumer is a moving target. Changes in the economy, demographics, and lifestyles can affect consumer demands. It is likely that several of these factors will change during a typical two- or three-year planning, development, and sale period for a residential community. Your marketing plan should be flexible enough to allow enhancement and refinement of the project throughout the development process.

Important elements of a marketing plan are outlined in Appendix A. This can serve as a planning document

Figure 68. Components of a Marketing Budget

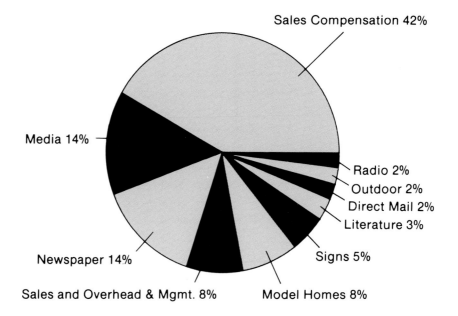

Sales Compensation 42%

Media 14%

Radio 2%

Outdoor 2%

Direct Mail 2%

Literature 3%

Signs 5%

Newspaper 14%

Sales and Overhead & Mgmt. 8%

Model Homes 8%

Figure 69. Components of House Price

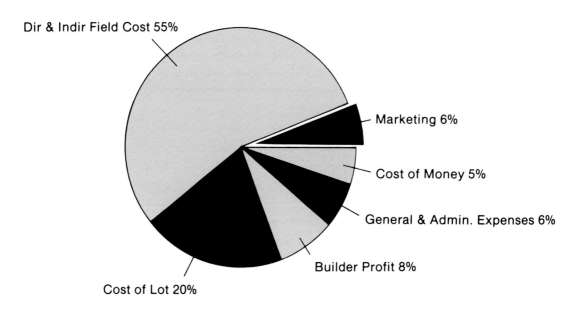

Dir & Indir Field Cost 55%

Marketing 6%

Cost of Money 5%

General & Admin. Expenses 6%

Builder Profit 8%

Cost of Lot 20%

The Goodkin Group

and control form. A project development checklist includes various development tasks which involve marketing decisions, as shown in Appendix B.

Budgets and Controls

Budgets provide a structure from which resources can be strategically allocated and monitored. Controls are necessary to protect profit. Budgets can vary dramatically, depending on the type of higher density product being built. General guidelines from which to determine budgets are shown in Figures 68-69.

It is important to remember that the development process is indeed a *process* to achieve a desired result: a marketable home. "Marketability" should be defined by research and analysis, which in turn dictates function, price, and design—a "market driven product." The development process—with profitability based on budgets—must be controlled as a means to achieve that goal.

Target Markets

Target markets are the core of the marketing plan. Weigh every action for its impact on the potential homebuyer audience. Methods for identifying target markets are discussed in the market research chapter of the Planning section. A comprehensive profile of buyer segments is also found in the market research chapter.

Traffic Goals

Product absorption is closely related to traffic.

- How many prospects should you target each week and how many can you close?
- How much will it cost to win over each prospect?
- How do you reach a qualified universe of prospects?
- How do you staff the sales office to maximize capture?

Market research and experience answer these questions. They can provide criteria for sales office design and staffing decisions as well.

Sales Goals

Be realistic in planning sales goals. A life-of-the-marketing-period absorption rate of two units per week probably won't equate to two units every week. Early selling efforts may yield higher sales rates; as inventory diminishes, your sales rate may decrease. Delays in processing loan documents and escrow closings often pose hidden threats to the overall sales rate. Some of these problems concern higher density communities especially, so consider how cash flow, staffing, and advertising can be affected.

Product Development

The builder must decide how to design a home based on the needs and wants of the target market. Product type, configuration, size, features, and common area amenities must be considered. This is the process of building a "market driven" product. Budgets and controls may play an important role during the product development process. They can answer such questions as: How much can I afford to spend on a house or amenity and still make a profit? Which designs and amenities give the most impact for the dollar? For example, many builders may find that their higher density developments benefit from emphasis on common areas and neighborhood amenities.

Pricing, Financing, and Phasing

These should be viewed as tools for implementing the market plan.

Pricing

This should not simply be remuneration for costs incurred plus profit. Goals of a pricing strategy include establishing project momentum, value reinforcement, motivation for immediate purchase, and increasing the sales velocity of selected units, plans, and phases.

Financing

Target markets may react differently to various financing strategies. Financing can increase affordability where qualification is difficult; however, some market segments may not respond. Selected-unit financing can be a tool to affect the relative sales velocity of units. Knowledge of the consumer is paramount in determining a financing strategy. A computer in the sales office is an invaluable financing tool, and has numerous other benefits as well.

Phasing

Flexibility in higher density housing can be enhanced with a phasing strategy, in which a project is developed and sold off in sections. This approach permits refinements in product throughout the development process. Phasing strategy considers absorption rates, unit mix, size of sales releases, and economics of production and construction financing. It can affect the overall project site plan, and may become complex with higher density development.

Merchandising and Presentation

A home should be developed according to a market-driven formula. Merchandising and presentation augment this process by appealing to buyer wants and needs through landscaping, furniture, accessories, color schemes, and printed information.

Offsite Signage and Displays

Billboards These should be low in copy, high in visibility. Effective locations may vary depending on product type. Major highways or arterials are often successful. For example, if your project's primary selling point is location relative to employment, a sign along heavily traveled commuter routes may be effective. Resort-oriented projects can advertise on billboards in metropolitan areas as well as on routes leading to and from the resort location, possibly interesting households that currently rent in those markets. A commuter-oriented billboard that has been successful for a San Diego builder is shown in Figure 70.

Displays in public areas describing the product in inviting words and pictures. Possible display locations include train stations and other public transportation centers, and shopping malls.

Figure 70. Billboard on a San Diego freeway exposes this project to a variety of buyer segments

The Goodkin Group

Figure 71. Directional sign leads prospects from public streets to community

Rancho Santa Margarita, Orange County, CA
Developer: Santa Margarita Company
Source: The Goodkin Group

Directional signs can be smaller than billboards, and are designed to lead prospects from public streets to your community (Figure 71). "Burma shave" signs with consecutive messages can also be effective.

Use your imagination to come up with other creative types of offsite signage. Hot air balloons, for example, stand out in a competitive market and can be cost-effective (Figure 72).

Onsite Signage and Displays

Entry monuments are important to higher density projects. Their purpose is to establish a feeling of self-contained community, particularly if the project is near a negative lead-in environment, such as an industrial area or poorer-quality housing.

Entry monuments should feature the community name, and should reflect quality and elegance even if the housing is low-priced. In a smaller project, the entry sign can serve as the monument if it has character to it, such as the use of unusual wood and eye-catching lettering or colors. Psychologically, a good entry monument connotes quality, seclusion, and community image to prospects (Figure 73).

Lead-in signs from entry to models while not necessary, are convenient and can be an attractive design element. Lead-in signs can serve two purposes: as directionals leading to the models, and as a listing of features and amenities prospects will get if they buy a home in the community.

Miscellaneous opportunities Even the perimeter construction fence around your project offers a chance to market in a unique fashion. Figure 74 shows caricatures painted on a fence viewing project construction, promoting anticipation of the community's opening.

Figure 72. Hot air balloon at the junction of two heavily traveled freeways gives unique exposure to a higher density project

The Goodkin Group

Figure 73. Entry monument establishes community identity

Rancho Santa Margarita, Orange County, CA
Developer: Santa Margarita Company
Source: The Goodkin Group

Figure 74. Creative use of perimeter fencing at a higher density construction site promotes anticipation

Cienega County Crossings, Tucson, AZ
Source: The Goodkin Group

Figure 75. Model identification sign reinforces Mediterranean project theme

The Goodkin Group

Models

The model is the prospect's first face-to-face contact with your product. Therefore, it should be positioned and designed to say *home* to those who visit it.

Location

The streetscape on which models are located should be designed to reflect what the community will look like on a typical street basis. The best location for models is not on top of the street entry, but set back slightly to give them a sense of individuality.

Each model should be named to enhance the feeling of identity. Have some sort of theme, such as mountains, lakes, artists, poets, or music. This theme may tie into the overall community name. Model identification signs reinforce project theme, as shown in Figure 75. Repeat the model name on signs inside the home, using signage material and lettering that expresses quality.

Landscaping

Plant landscaping between model units for privacy, and to soften and enhance elevations. There must be greenery even in winter, and a riot of color during spring, summer, and fall.

Don't forget to landscape all side and back yards. Work leisure activities into the model's landscape design: barbeques, potsheds, patios with colorful outdoor furniture. Create a lifestyle your target markets can relate to. Offer to bring your decorator and landscapers in to talk to buyers and give them additional ideas.

Parking

Parking areas should be defined, but should be landscaped to soften their impact on the streetscape. If on-street parking is used, make sure that it is not located directly in front of models. Otherwise, the effectiveness of well-designed model elevations and landscaping will be lost. Whatever parking system is used, the lead-in to models should be direct.

Inside the Model

It is recommended that each model be decorated to appeal to a specific market segment. Give each room an identity for a male, female, child, teenager, or retiree—someone that prospects can relate to.

Overcome consumer concerns about space restrictions in higher density housing by showing flexibility in room usage—especially in the extra bedroom, den, utility room, loft, hallway, or stairway landing. Be clever in your space planning and merchandise it heavily. Showcase closets, storage, pantries, shelving—even garages (Figure 76).

Don't be afraid to use textures, colors, furniture, artwork, and plants to create a reaction. Remember that you are sparking prospects' imaginations—making the home come alive for them—regardless of price or size. If a patio or deck is part of the design, incorporate it into the home itself to increase the perception of total usable space (Figure 77).

The NAHB videotape, *Money-Making Models: Selling through Design,* gives viewers an onsite tour of three well-designed models, each targeted to a different market segment.

Maintain model areas so that they look fresh and new. And keep all finished inventory clean. No matter how good your product is, it won't sell if it's shabby-looking or dirty. Devise a monitoring system to keep track of housekeeping, and assign specific personnel to maintain models and inventory.

Figure 76. Showcase features that demonstrate spaciousness or luxury: glass door draws prospects' attention to the spacious garage

The Goodkin Group

Figure 77. Patio view adds visual excitement to master suite and increases space perception

The Goodkin Group

Advertising

Advertising begins with media research. What outlets are available to reach the higher density audience? What do they read? Listen to?

Newspapers and Magazines

Consider placing ads in the following:

- Newspapers
  Real estate section
  Financial section
  Sports and television sections
  Classified section
  Small community newspapers
- Home and garden magazines
- New home selling magazines (these are a good, steady source of traffic)

Radio and Television

Radio can be effective for certain target segments, such as those that can be reached in their cars during commuter hour. Classical and "beautiful" music stations can efficiently reach mature households and empty-nesters; nostalgia-oriented light rock stations appeal to the young professional audience.

Television has been successful in reaching the seniors market, and should be considered as advertising budget and target audience permit. In areas where it is available, cable television offers a cost-effective, market-specific alternative to network TV advertising.

Direct Mail

Direct mail is an important advertising tool. It offers an opportunity to efficiently reach a target audience and reduce advertising costs. The direct mail campaign should be well planned and carefully executed to appeal to higher density buyers. Direct mail pieces must be designed to make recipients curious enough to read and respond. This requires ingenuity on the part of advertising/design staff.

Direct mail should contain factual information about the community, but don't be afraid to use vivid language to describe lifestyle and amenities.

Many builders experiment with direct mail, but give up on it too quickly because they expect immediate results. Don't become discouraged and don't keep changing the direct mail piece. Allow time to test it. Remember that direct mail does not pull immediately and dramatically like an ad can. It may take several mailings to the same list before the campaign pays off.

You should be building up your own mailing list from the time you first announce your project. All signs and company literature should include your telephone number. The names and addresses of all callers should be recorded—they will form the basis of your direct mail list. (Make sure all company personnel that answer the telephone have a printed sheet with project data to refer to. This ensures that all callers receive the same information). These "early interest" lists can be analyzed for consumer segmentation, and each segment can be targeted in subsequent advertising.

After your project opens, a guest register should be maintained. This allows you to contact prospects with continuous updates on new unit releases, pricing, and financing changes. Sharp salespeople will note specific needs and characteristics of prospects and can personalize follow-up messages.

Mailing lists can also be purchased from commercial list houses for whatever categories of people you request. Consult your *Yellow Pages* for mailing list suppliers.

Many builders are turning to "rifle shot" advertising. This is the process of communicating to specific target markets or households that have been prequalified for function and price. Proper implementation of rifle shot advertising requires thorough knowledge of target segments. This can increase front-end research costs but will substantially reduce actual advertising costs. Capture ratio may increase as a result of rifle shot advertising.

Advertising Phases

The development of a higher density project goes through specific phases, which are identified below. The advertising strategy must be programmed to correspond to these phases.

- Pre-sale (before models are completed)
- Preview
- Grand opening
- Sustaining

- Cleaning up inventory
- Grand closing

Advertising costs can run from one to one-and-a-half percent of the home sale price. Don't spend too much of the advertising budget before models are ready to show. Remember that the longer buyers have to wait between making a deposit on the home and actually purchasing it, the greater the chance they will cancel the order.

For example, advertising during the pre-sale phase can take the form of onsite billboards, publicity, and some selective direct mail to former buyers and drop-bys. Save the bulk of the ad budget for when the project is at its best.

Designing Ads

Advertisements for higher density communities should feature a project theme around which the campaign can focus. For example:

- Environmental feature (Lakeside)
- Nature (The Meadows)
- Location (Cleveland Heights)
- Foreign name or style (Le Parc)
- Lifestyle (Golfview)
- Builder/developer trade name (K & B's Eastglen)
- Architecture (Manor Villas)

Ads should play up lifestyle, location, product style, price and terms. Pictures are an effective means of illustrating these points. Remember that photographs tend to look better in magazines and can reproduce poorly on newsprint.

Since most real estate ads look alike, special attention should be given to making yours stand out. Use eye-catching borders, bold words, clever cartoons and caricatures, or color. Color is especially effective in ads for higher density projects. For example, greens and blues can be used to suggest green open space and blue skies. Ads for large-scale projects should hit the reader with dramatic effects, size, and color. Smaller projects should be advertised with well-written copy to dramatize amenities and character (Figure 78).

Using an Advertising Agency

Some companies may prefer to use an outside agency instead of handling advertising in-house. This gives builder/developers flexibility to select an agency whose specialties match the demands of individual projects or target markets. Using an outside agency may also keep in-house staff overhead costs down. A form for communicating project information to an advertising agency is shown in Appendix C.

While front-end costs may be higher with an outside agency, sales may increase as agencies apply sophisticated research, analysis, and advertising techniques. The consumer information generated can provide better insights for targeting product to market.

Figure 78. Newspaper real estate ads should dramatize a community's character and amenities

The Goodkin Group

Promotion

Promotions are special events designed to draw traffic to your community and generate good publicity. Crowds create an image of activity, excitement, desirability, and success. Promotions should always be sales oriented. Attracting a crowd is worthless if the sales team isn't equipped to handle it.

Successful promotions require planning and ingenuity. They must have their own budgets and must be rehearsed in every detail. They should showcase elegance, happiness, and freedom of lifestyle, rather than simply create traffic.

Budgets

Promotional budgets may vary depending on the anticipated response of targeted homebuying segments. Is the competitive market flooded with promotions, or is it an unsophisticated market where creative promotional activities will set your project apart from the competition?

An average promotional allowance is 2 percent of the marketing budget; however, this varies substantially depending on the size of the project and the scope of competitive promotional strategies.

Promotional Ideas

Nighttime promotions can be especially effective. The use of afterdark is convenient for many prospects and it connotes sophistication as well. Assign a single individual to coordinate the event, or leave it in the hands of your advertising agency (if you use one).

Promotions should be designed to generate interest among the market segments you are building for (Figure 79). Among the themes that work for different groups:

- Sports shows and action
- Winetasting and gourmet
- Celebrity appearances
- Financial planning programs
- Tie-in with a local department store
- Homemaking, baking, cooking
- Gimmicks, such as hot air balloons (Figure 72)

Follow-Through

Every promotion must include follow-through. Establish a company follow-through system, so that salespeople know how to follow up every lead gained during the promotional event. A three-part follow-up

Figure 79. A promotional party during grand opening week at Laguna Meadows, a 120-townhome project in Orange County, CA

The Goodkin Group
Photography: Smetona

is good: the Monday after the event, the Thursday of the same week, and the next Thursday. A prospect follow-through form is shown in Figure 80.

Plan a direct mail piece to all leads gained from the promotion, to be sent immediately after the event. This should be followed by telephone calls to all leads and direct mail recipients. Try to get people back for a second visit to the community.

Sales

Sales is the art—and science—of converting customer interest into a commitment to buy. Without an effective sales approach, all of the marketing strategies discussed so far are useless.

The Sales Team

If your organization is small, hire a solid broker who will staff the sales office with a full range of sales and administrative skills. Make sure the broker has sold higher density homes before. A two-or-more person office can have a manager with sales and administrative responsibilities, and one or more salespeople. A salesperson with administrative responsibility should get additional (noncommission) compensation for his/her efforts. Nothing is more important than having a sales team that is fully prepared to sell. Money spent on market research, product development, and advertising pays off with the sales function.

The Project Sales Manager

The sales team is directed by the project sales manager, who generally reports to the project man-

ager or director of marketing. The project sales manager can be either an in-house employee or an outside contractor who provides various levels of service to complement in-house sales activities.

Responsibilities of the project sales manager include:

- Policy development
- Recruiting
- Training
- Daily management and reporting
- Presenting community features as consumer benefits
- Financial analysis
- Management of credit and loan processing procedures
- Development and monitoring of a staff sales manual
- Recommendation of new sales policies and procedures to management
- Other tasks as directed by management

Salespeople

Good salespeople know how to promote the benefits of the product they are selling. They know what the competition is doing and how to match buyer needs to available product. Consumers will buy from salespeople they trust.

What are the characteristics of good salespeople? They should:

- communicate well
- think on their feet
- be "hungry" and ambitious
- organize their time well

Figure 80. Prospect Follow-Through Form

Week Ending: _____

Name	Address	Phone No.	Called	Called	Called	Mailed	Results

Salesman: _____   Route to: _____
_____
The Goodkin Group

- have a satisfying hobby away from work
- be people-oriented extroverts
- have a high degree of self-confidence
- be goal-oriented individuals

Sales Training

The sales function revolves around seven vital skills:

Prospecting This is the art of finding qualified buyers. It involves attracting prospects by means other than advertising and promotional programs, locating buyers and approaching them directly. For example, first-time buyers can be found in upscale apartment projects. "Away-from-site" prospecting is very important: encourage salespeople to go beyond the sales office in developing contacts. There are no sales without prospects.

Approach The salesperson's approach sets the tone for a working relationship with the prospect. Sales personnel should rehearse methods of approaching prospects in various situations.

Qualifying The salesperson has an opportunity to qualify buyers prior to demonstrating the product.

This includes qualification of function (which product model does this household need?) as well as financial qualification.

Demonstration Each project has special, positive characteristics that should be personally conveyed by a salesperson. Encourage salespeople to qualify prospects in a model based on that home's function, then personally walk them through inventory, "selling" the benefits of other models.

Demonstration gives the salesperson an opportunity to spend more time with a prospect and better understand his/her needs. If the prospect can visualize family, furniture, and lifestyle in the product you've demonstrated, an emotional bond is created among salesperson, prospect, and community.

Many higher density projects feature common areas requiring payment of an association fee. Demonstration of common area facilities and benefits can be important in justifying association fees to the prospect.

The NAHB videotape, *How to Demonstrate a Model Home,* offers an onsite look at effective model home demonstration.

Overcoming objections and rejection Salespeople should be trained to overcome objections presented by prospects. An objection such as, *The closets are too small,* can be countered with the response, *We have allocated extra space to the living area and provided finished space in the attic for additional storage.* Rejection can have a similar response, such as, *Let me show you the two-bedroom model. You may prefer the floor plan.*

Strategies for overcoming objection and rejection can be planned in advance, based on the characteristics of individual projects.

Closing Other than prospecting, closing can be the most important skill acquired by a salesperson. Salespeople should be very familiar with strategies for how, when, and where to close. Plans for overcoming objection and rejection are also important in the closing process.

Service Servicing the buyer after a deposit is taken can reduce sales fallouts and increase buyer referrals. After-sales service can overcome "buyer remorse" and take advantage of the pride and enthusiasm generally associated with a new home purchase. Remember that friends and coworkers of recent, satisfied purchasers are potential homebuyers.

Train sales personnel regularly on selling lifestyle and amenities. A common problem with many salespeople is that they are not familiar enough with the products they are selling. They have not walked through the units, do not comprehend the subtleties of plans and locations. Each salesperson should receive a guided "tour" of every unit that is currently available for sale. Point out specific attributes of each room in each unit, such as a flowering tree that can be seen from a bedroom window. The salesperson will then be able to play these features up to prospects. The more individuality each home possesses, the more desirable it will seem to the buyer.

The sales team should understand that standing inventory kills profits. One common problem with builder marketing is that it responds to crises rather than being a preplanned strategy. An effective marketing plan will anticipate inventory patterns. The sales team must be able to focus on finished inventory when it is available. This means setting goals each weekend to get rid of certain units.

Each salesperson should be debriefed on Monday mornings to see what he/she has learned during the past week from and about advertising, that week's prospects and traffic survey, condition of inventory, financing, and new sales techniques. Thus, sales personnel become contributing members of the overall project team and staff learn from one another.

Compensate the sales team in accordance with market rates, but always give them an incentive to sell better. Incentive is not just money. It is an emotional reward too. Compensation is generally about 2.5 percent of the project budget; however, this figure varies considerably depending on region and economic conditions.

The Sales Office

The purpose of the sales office is to give salespeople and prospects an environment that is conducive to working and shopping for a new home. The sales office should always be identified on the outside as *Sales Office* or *Information Center.* It should feature a welcome sign and the project and builder name.

How to Locate the Sales Office

The sales office can take many forms. Among the more common are:

- The "trap." The sales office is located so that prospects have to go through it to get into and out of models. This gives sales personnel two opportunities to make contact: at entry and exit.
- A freestanding, free-flow structure that is not a trap.
- The garage of one of the models.
- An actual unit that has been decorated inside as a sales office.

Make sure that the sales office is easily accessible to customers. Models should be visible from the sales office, if possible, to give customers a point of reference as they talk with sales personnel. Locate the sales office near amenities for environmental and emotional impact. Give sales personnel a view of the parking lot so that they can "pre-qualify" prospects as they get out of their cars, and plan the sales approach.

Inside the Sales Office

The sales office should have a welcoming area where customers can relax, review project literature, and fill out research forms. This area should be located at some distance from the door to avoid crowding at the point of entry. Hire a host/hostess to staff the welcoming area, as a friendly face to greet customers as they enter and to hand out project literature.

Use the sales office to conduct onsite customer research. This can consist of short forms that the host/hostess or prospect fills out, containing name, address, phone, which model the customer liked best, intent to buy.

Environment in the sales office is important. Remember that you are selling a home *plus* a neighborhood. Prospects will want assurance that their investment will maintain its value or appreciate, so sell the community (Figure 81).

Sales personnel should have a desk or table as a work station. A table—preferably round—is better since it does not pose the barrier that a desk connotes. Customers expect to see salespeople so there is no need to hide their work stations. Wherever sales personnel are located, they should have a clear view of prospects as they enter the sales office.

Be sure to provide a private closing area. The decision to buy a home is an important and very

Figure 81. This sales office uses wall graphics to promote the geographic attributes of the community

The Goodkin Group

Figure 82. Orientation map in sales office

The Goodkin Group

personal one for most people, and one that should be made in privacy. Any discussion of personal finances should take place in this comfortable private area.

Don't forget to allow for storage space in the sales office. Project literature, signs, and office supplies should be hidden from view.

Sales Tools

Every sales office should be equipped with "tools" designed to introduce prospects to the project and sell them on the advantages of buying there. Among the selling tools you should consider:

- Orientation map—or better, an aerial photo—showing the location of the project within the larger community. Include shopping (names of major department stores and supermarkets), recreational areas, cultural facilities, schools and universities, highways. The emphasis should be on access and convenience (Figures 82-83).
- Builder story. Make a distinction between you and the others who are building higher density. The builder's background and experience must be clearly illustrated with pictures and descriptions of other projects he/she has built, whether commercial or residential. The prospect must have a sense of competence and trust in your work.
- A topographic model or replica of the development, showing scope and theme. Indicate the overall land plan and plots of each unit in the project. Use special flags to mark each home that has sold.
- Street scene of typical elevations in the community.
- Floor plans and features of each model. Emphasize any luxury items that are standard in each type of model. Highlight quality details in your homes that the prospect may not be able to see, or that are hidden by construction. Remember that durability and dependability are important selling points.
- Lifestyle. Show prospects the benefits of living here. Show them amenities that make the project

Figure 83. Aerial photograph in sales office and other sales office tools

The Goodkin Group

a community: action pictures of people like them doing things they like to do, such as walking, talking, swimming, resting, playing games and sports. Convey a sense of both privacy and community. Don't be afraid to sell romance and elegance. Just because the project may be at market entry pricing doesn't mean your audience doesn't want "the finer things in life." Keep in mind that today's buyers have many leisure-time options available to them. Sell them what *your* community has to offer.

- Buying versus renting. Illustrate the benefits of buying over renting, especially to the first-time-buyer market. Your salespeople must be educated to address this point knowledgeably. Have an accountant work up the figures. Then train your sales team to use a flip chart or computer to illustrate the financial advantages of homeownership to prospects. Emphasize the concepts of investment, lifestyle, roots, raising children, place of retirement, equity build-up (as another way of saving), and tax benefits.

Consider using displays that make you unique—that the prospect will remember. Explore the use of television, audio-visuals, a small theatre for sit-down viewing, oversized graphics to tell the project story, fountains, dramatic indoor landscaping.

Sales Literature

The brochure is a selling tool that merits a full discussion of its own. It is the only tangible item that an undecided prospect can carry away and pore over—the "take home" pitch that covers everything

sales personnel have (or have not) already explained. It is the ultimate reinforcement for the prospect to review in the privacy of car or present home (Figure 84).

The brochure should retell the builder story, emphasizing quality and experience. Mention the convenient location—schools, shopping facilities, parks, cultural attractions that are nearby. And don't forget to feature lifestyle. Include elevations, a list of standard amenities, floor plans that show furniture placement. Most buying segments have an existing house filled with furniture that they must arrange in their new home. An oversized (16" × 20") set of floorplans allows prospects to sketch their belongings into your models.

Brochures are typically given to prospects as they enter the sales office and are greeted by a host/hostess or salesperson. Some salespeople withhold the brochure or a portion of the sales literature until after a prospect has viewed the models. This can irritate some customers, however, who prefer to see prices, floorplans, and descriptions as they walk through homes.

Figure 84. Use the take-home brochure as a final sales pitch: feature lifestyle, amenities, and builder/developer reputation

Rancho Santa Margarita, Orange County, CA
Developer: Santa Margarita Group
Source: The Goodkin Group

THE URBAN VILLAGE: TOWN OF TOMORROW.

Rancho Santa Margarita is being built according to a plan that will make it unusual even when the next century unfolds. It is a town master-planned as a totally self-sufficient "Urban Village"—a concept so new that it requires explanation to be truly understood.

Its concept is "Urban" because—when com-

pleted—it would combine virtually all the elements and advantages found in a small city: broad housing variety, a business center, a town center, neighborhood shopping centers, plus extensive recreational, civic, cultural and commercial resources.

It is a "Village" because all of these elements

ARTIST'S CONCEPTION

8

Rancho Santa Margarita, Orange County, CA
Developer: Santa Margarita Group
Source: The Goodkin Group

HOMES FOR PEOPLE IN ALL STAGES OF LIFE.

The homes and apartments in the first phase of the town have not been planned for a few, but for the many.

For people in all stages of life. Single. Married. Families. The young. The mid years. The later years. People at various income levels and with all sorts of preferences.

To meet these needs, housing in a variety of types and prices has been created:

- Garden apartments for those just starting out...
- Smaller, single-family attached homes for first-time buyers...
- Larger, more spacious attached homes for people moving up...
  ...all with their own neighborhood recreation centers.
- Also, detached homes in a range of sizes—for people with growing families or a taste for space.

Housing and public buildings in the town are being designed to incorporate an overall architectural theme reminiscent of the grace and style of early California architecture. Stucco. Tile roofs. Patios. Porches. Arbors. Bells. Touches from the past. And landscaping of community streets, parks and open space has been designed not just for appearance sake, but to heighten the experience of living here.

All to carry forward the heritage and traditions of Early California...to make them an integral part of the town. And to provide a sense of community and homestead for its residents.

~

Give me something to see at daybreak.
Something to run to when I come home.
Something for my mind. My need to get away.
Give me a place with space.

Rancho Santa Margarita was created for people with feelings like these.

BRISA DEL LAGO
Single-Family Attached Homes by Baywood Homes

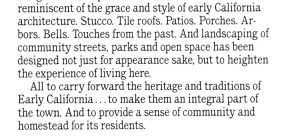

EL CASERIO
Single-Family Detached Homes by The Fieldstone Company

CANTOBRIO
Single-Family Detached Homes by The Fieldstone Company

FLORAMAR
Single-Family Attached Homes by Century American Corporation

ARTIST'S CONCEPTIONS are based on actual architectural building plans provided by each builder.

NOTE: The Rancho Santa Margarita Landscape and Recreation Corporation has been established to enhance the long-term value and integrity of the community. It provides a vehicle for maintaining community recreation and common areas. The organization is financially supported by all residents of Rancho Santa Margarita. Membership is automatic.

Rancho Santa Margarita, Orange County, CA
Developer: Santa Margarita Group
Source: The Goodkin Group

Traffic and Sales Analysis

Traffic and sales analysis play a crucial role in control of the marketing plan. Traffic analysis can provide important feedback on advertising efficiency. What is the cost per prospect? Are qualified buyers being attracted, or should refinements in advertising media be made?

Sales analysis complements traffic analysis. Adver-

tising effectiveness can be measured by assessing which media or promotions draw traffic versus actual sales. A master control sheet can track this information weekly. Prospect report forms are an important tool for salespeople and sales managers to use in tracking and following up on potential homebuyers (Figures 85-86).

Figure 85. Prospect Report

Development _____

Salesperson _____ Date _____

Prospect's name _____ Telephone (____) _____

Street _____ City _____

State _____ Zip _____

Model liked best _____ Location of employment _____

Reason for not buying now _____

_____

Other comments _____

_____

_____

The Goodkin Group

Figure 86. Prospect Follow-Up Report

Development _____

Salesperson _____ Date _____

Prospect's name _____

Date first visited site _____

Dates of contacts (phone, mail or additional visits)

_____   _____   _____

_____   _____   _____

Type of contact(s) made _____

No. of contacts made _____

No. of children ____ Now own ____ rent ____ other ____

Present monthly payment $_____

Why wanting to move _____

_____

_____

Where first learned about development _____

Model preferred _____ Why _____

Reason for not buying _____

_____

_____

Other comments _____

_____

_____

The Goodkin Group

Public Relations

Public relations is a means of disseminating information in a planned and consistent manner. A broad range of groups can be reached with information complementing other marketing efforts. Public relations goals include:

- Establishing and maintaining a reputation for building quality product.
- Creating a consistent image to appear in all communications, letterhead, and other literature. The press is becoming more sophisticated; your company must recognize this and capitalize on it. A reliable company spokesperson should be designated.
- Creation of a corporate posture in community and lifestyle issues. A growing, maturing company needs to make its community and philanthropic presence felt.
- Maintaining and improving relationships with fiduciaries and the building industry by projecting the image of a solid, reliable, public-minded and forward-thinking company.
- Distinct but complementary public relations programs for the company and its subsidiaries, where applicable.

Public relations should be handled by a professional, on or off staff, who is very familiar with the project. It should be coordinated with the advertising campaign. Regular quarterly meetings of all professionals involved with a project can assure continuity between public relations and other components of the marketing plan. Chart out the public relations program in advance, so that your stories correspond with regular weekly or monthly features in the local press. Figure 87 shows a typical publicity schedule, which can be adapted to your particular project.

Develop a fact sheet on your community that tells what the project is and where it is, who is the target market, and why they should live there. This should be a staple part of your press kit, so keep it up to date. It does not have to be anything fancy—just neat.

Other public relations stories could address:

- The history of higher density housing in America, or in your area
- Townhome or villa living
- The new markets that are choosing a higher density lifestyle (first-time buyers, young profes-

Figure 87. Typical Publicity Schedule

1. Property purchased
2. Development plans announced
3. Development features announced
4. Development supervisor announced
5. Architect named
6. Subcontractor named
7. Number of house plans listed
8. Recreational facility advisor named
9. Development aimed at target market
10. Development community master plan announced
11. Recreational facilities described
12. Sales agent or sales manager appointed
13. Groundbreaking ceremonies announced
14. Home features described (expand to several stories) TV/radio/special promotions and coverage organized
15. Sneak preview announcement sent out
16. Pre-opening ceremonies announced
17. Pre-completion sales announced
18. First unit type sold out prior to opening models
19. Model homes near completion
20. Grand opening planned to feature special event
21. Grand opening today
22. First home sold
23. First move-ins
24. Financing plans described— FHA, VA, No Down Payment, etc.
25. Park site dedicated
26. Sales ahead of projection
27. Grand opening of second unit type
28. Model X is best seller
29. Special event today
30. Development 50 percent sold
31. Award received
32. Sales set record
33. Two models seesaw in popularity
34. Sellout near
35. Models for sale
36. Sale close

The Goodkin Group

sionals, empty-nesters, retirees, and so on)
- Efficient space planning and decorating ideas for higher density living

The public relations program is much more than publicity. It is also:

- Community relations
- Internal communication with company personnel (often in the form of a newsletter)
- Community association relations, where applicable (may require a full-or part-time staff person)
- Local government relations

Post-Sale Relations

Purpose

Many home buyers feel that all the builder wants is the money once the house is sold. Too many times it certainly looks that way—not because that's what the builder wants, but because he/she has neglected to plan for customer relations after the sale.

Pre-Move-In

Customer satisfaction should begin before the sale even closes. Give new buyers a move-in kit explaining how the community association works, what their responsibilities will be for upkeep and repair, any warranties that apply to their home. Change-of-address cards and a home repair booklet (such as NAHB's *Your New Home and How to Take Care of It*) are nice touches.

Get buyers involved in the community before they move in. This is particularly wise while the project is under construction. Send buyers a newsletter that tells who is buying homes there, describes the status of construction, landscaping and amenities, and features testimonials from local media and the surrounding community.

Involve them in promotions. Invite them to participate in a design seminar, or to meet with a designer who can assist them in color selection and upgrades. Upgrades should be offered as a feature of any higher density housing above the entry-level market. Getting the buyer to plan upgrades and home improvements before even moving in is a sure way to discourage cancellations.

Post-Move-In

Once buyers have moved in, continue to show that you're glad they chose to live in your community. Flowers, a fruit basket, or a bottle of wine awaiting the buyer on move-in day create good will and are an inexpensive way to say "welcome."

Make the good will last by establishing a "listening" mechanism that is attentive to the needs of all residents. There should be a central place to register complaints, and a well-organized response system. Arrange to get a weekly report on the status of all service calls. Always answer a complaint promptly—even to report no progress. The resident needs to feel attended to. Remember that while good news travels fast, bad news—such as dissatisfaction with the builder—will travel even faster through the community. Disarm it with fast, efficient service. Be known as a fair and responsive builder. Referrals from satisfied customers can be one of the most effective marketing tools a builder has.

Post-Sale Management

One often-overlooked aspect of marketing management is the salesperson's role in loan processing, relations with take-out lenders and escrow companies, and the overall coordination of these elements. A sales-to-closing log can be very useful.

Profit is often lost because of poor post-sale management. For example, an overworked sales manager may not be able to process and manage loan documents efficiently. If the paperwork phase is delayed, additional interest must be carried which reduces profit. Building post-sale management into the standard sales staff workload allows personnel to plan their time more efficiently.

In summary, marketing is everybody's responsibility. It requires teamwork for efficiency and effectiveness. The process begins at project conception, and almost every decision made throughout the development process has marketing implications. A good marketing plan will pay off both in increased sales and in the community goodwill your project generates.

Appendix A

Marketing Plan Checklist

Source: The Greenman Group, Inc.

1. ANALYSIS

NOTES:

- [ ] A. Market Research, Definition and Analysis
- [ ] B. Site Analysis
- [ ] C. Feasibility Analysis (Budget, Product Mix, Pricing, Amenities, etc.)
- [ ] D. Consumer/Market Profile
- [ ] E. Analysis of Existing Project (Merchandising, Sales, Cosmetics, Pricing, Advertising, Presentation, etc.) for New, Tired or Distressed Properties
- [ ] F. Analysis of Competitive Projects (Merchandising, Cosmetics, Sales, Pricing, Advertising, Presentation, etc.)
- [ ] G. Analysis of Floorplans and Elevations (Units, Amenities, Recreation Facilities, Sales Center, Day Care, Welcome Center, etc.)
- [ ] H. Project Name and Logo Selection and/or Review
- [ ] I. Analysis of Sales Staff and Procedures
- [ ] J. Input Session with Marketing/Creative Team
- [ ] K. Shop Sales Offices/Personnel

2. FORECASTING

- [ ] A. Define Target Audience/Market Area/Demographics
- [ ] B. Marketing Strategy/Objectives

3. BUDGETING

- [ ] A. Marketing/Merchandising/Advertising/Promotional Budgets

Input / Preliminary / Presentation / Pre-production / Production Complete / Completion Delivery Install

120

		Input	Preliminary	Presentation	Pre-production	Production Complete	Completion Delivery Install
☐	B. Media Analysis Budgets						
☐	C. Cash Flow Projections (Media Production)						
☐	D. Reserves. Contingencies and misc.						

4. CORPORATE DESIGN

☐	A. Corporate Image Identity						
☐	B. Name						
☐	C. Logotype						
☐	D. Slogan						
☐	E. Trademark						
☐	F. Project Master Color Materials Specifications						
☐	G. Typographic Styling						

5. STATIONERY / FORMAT

☐	A. Letterhead						
☐	B. Envelopes						
☐	C. Business Cards						
☐	D. Mailing Labels						
☐	E. Direct Mail Form Letters. Follow-ups. etc.						
☐	F. Postage Meter Imprint						
☐	G. Unit Traffic Report						

Input
Preliminary
Presentation
Pre-production
Production Complete
Completion Delivery Install

		Input	Preliminary	Presentation	Pre-production	Production Complete	Completion Delivery Install
☐	H Unit Sales / Productivity / Conversion Information Forms						
☐	I Leases Condo Documents, etc.						
☐	J Move-In Notice (Change of Address)						
☐	K Informal Note Stationery						
☐	L All Related Forms						

6. CREATIVE

		Input	Preliminary	Presentation	Pre-production	Production Complete	Completion Delivery Install
☐	A Design Layout						
☐	B Copy						
☐	C Master Photography 1) Color 2) Black & White						
☐	D Stat Type Specification						
☐	E Stat Type Composition						
☐	F Renderings, Illustrations						
☐	G Paste-Up & Mechanicals						

7. MEDIA

		Input	Preliminary	Presentation	Pre-production	Production Complete	Completion Delivery Install
☐	A Media Research						
☐	B Local Newspapers						
☐	1) Display						
☐	2) Classified						
☐	3) Special Sections						

		Input	Preliminary	Presentation	Pre-production	Production Complete	Completion/Delivery/Install
☐	C. Television						
☐	D. Radio						
☐	E. Outdoor Media (Painted Board, Junior Board, Paper Posting, Bus Bench)						
☐	F. Specialized Outdoor Indoor Advertising (Aerial Signs, Sky Writing, Balloons, etc.)						
☐	G. Direct Mail (Specialized Lists & Materials)						
☐	H. National Local Yellow Pages						
☐	I. National Consumer Magazines/Newspapers						
☐	J. National Trade Magazines/Newspapers						
☐	K. Bus (Interior, Exterior)						
☐	L. Taxi						
☐	M. Airport						
☐	1) Island Displays						
☐	2) Billboards						
☐	3) Dioramas						
☐	4) Taxis/Limousines						
☐	N. Hotel/Motel Displays						
☐	O. Other Local, National, Regional, Target or Specialized Media						

8. TEMPORARY SIGNAGE / GRAPHICS   NOTES:

		Input	Preliminary	Presentation	Pre-production	Production Complete	Completion/Delivery/Install
☐	A. Off-Site Road Directionals / Curb Bootlegs (50% Straight Ahead, 25% Left, 25% Right)						
☐	B. Site Boundary Identification						
☐	C. On-Site Marketing Directionals						
☐	D. Parking Controls						
☐	E. Sales Site Identification						
☐	F. Welcome Center Signage						
☐	G. Model Site Informationals, Disclaimers, Directionals & Talkers						
☐	H. Excavation and Construction Barriers						
☐	I. Future Amenity Locations / Identifications						

9. PERMANENT SIGNAGE / GRAPHICS

		Input	Preliminary	Presentation	Pre-production	Production Complete	Completion/Delivery/Install
☐	A. Master Boundary and Frontage Graphics						
☐	B. Master Entry Graphics						
☐	C. Street Signage						
☐	D. Street Lighting						
☐	E. Street Furniture						
☐	F. Directionals						
☐	G. Project Recognition						

		Input	Preliminary	Presentation	Pre-production	Production Complete	Completion/Delivery/Install
☐	H. Village & Building Identification						
☐	I. Club/Site Directory & Signage						
☐	J. Interior Directory or Signage (Library, Laundry, etc.)						
☐	K. Flags						

10. SALES CENTER PLANNING, DESIGN AND COORDINATION
(Interior & Exterior)

		Input	Preliminary	Presentation	Pre-production	Production Complete	Completion/Delivery/Install
☐	A. Traffic Flow/Program						
☐	1) Identification Signage						
☐	2) Directional Signage						
☐	3) Parking and Entry						
☐	4) Reception and Information						
☐	5) Internal Patterns & Holding Areas (Normal & Peak Load)						
☐	B. Exterior Design						
☐	1) Facade						
☐	2) Landscaping						
☐	3) Parking						
☐	4) Flags and Banners						
☐	C. Display Space/Volume Design Requirements						
☐	1) Interior Display System & Design						
☐	a) Window Display						

NOTES:

	Item	Input	Preliminary	Presentation	Pre-production	Production Complete	Completion Delivery Install
☐	b) Display Panels						
☐	(1) Welcome Panel						
☐	(2) Corporate Image Panel (Builder Credibility)						
☐	(3) Location & Area Map & Features						
☐	(4) Lifestyle Photo Panels						
☐	(5) Homeowner's or Condo Association Panel						
☐	(6) Financial Investment Panel						
☐	(7) Building Plan Panel						
☐	(8) Floor Plan Selector						
☐	(9) Standard & Optional Features						
☐	(10) Key Product and Quality Panel						
☐	(11) Selection Board						
☐	(12) Model (Interior Design, Landscaping, Patio/Disclaimer)						
☐	(13) Unit Availability/Sold Board						
☐	(14) Amenity Story						
☐	(15) Security Story						
☐	(16) Elevations/Renderings						
☐	(17) Publicity Pin-Up Panels						
☐	c) Site Plans/Dioramas						

NOTES:

		Input	Preliminary	Presentation	Pre-production	Production Complete	Completion/Delivery/Install
☐	d) Architectural, Topographical, Mass, Scale & Diagrammatic Models						
☐	e) Interior Furnishings, Materials, Colors & Finishes						
☐	f) Theatre and/or Audio-Visual Techniques						
☐	g) Sales Stations (Normal & Peak)						
☐	h) Closing Rooms (Normal & Peak)						
☐	i) Literature Racks, Distribution & Storage						
☐	j) Selection Center for Appliances, Materials, Colors						
☐	k) Administrative Offices						
☐	l) Private Employee Lounge Area						
☐	m) Kitchen/Refreshment Area						
☐	n) Sales/Secretarial Area						
☐	o) General Storage Area						
☐	p) Public Lounge & Waiting Rooms						
☐	q) Public Rest Rooms, Fountains, Coat Room & Other Facilities						
☐	r) Children's Facilities (Tot Lot, Nursery, etc.)						
☐	s) Sales Personnel Uniforms/Costumes						
☐	t) Code Requirements Signage (No Smoking, Men's, Ladies', Exit, Entrance, Occupying Limits, etc.)						

		Input	Preliminary	Presentation	Pre-production	Production Complete	Completion Delivery Install
☐	u) Sound System (Intercom)						
☐	v) Security System						
☐	w) Mechanical Room						
☐	x) Conference Room						
☐	y) Reception Area						

11. COLLATERAL MATERIALS

☐	A. Brochure (Major, Minor)						
☐	B. Brochure (Rack, Direct Mail)						
☐	C. Project Feature and/or Amenities Folder						
☐	D. Site-Plan						
☐	E. Building/Amenity Plans						
☐	F. Unit Floorplans						
☐	G. Furniture Templates or "Punch-Outs"						
☐	H. Newsletter (Name, Format, Masthead)						
☐	I. Mortgage Presentation						
☐	J. Price Lists						
☐	K. Guarantees & Warranties						
☐	L. Sales Information (ie. Maintenance/Condo Ownership) and/or Related Reprints						

NOTES:

		Input	Preliminary	Presentation	Pre-production	Production Complete	Completion/Delivery/Install
☐	M. Tax Savings Computation Forms						
☐	N. Projection Forms, Labels, etc.						
☐	O. Developer Corporate Information						
☐	P. Real Estate Management Information						
☐	Q. Sales Contract						
☐	R. Sales Kits, Aids, Presentations						
☐	S. Sales Manuals, Data Books, etc.						
☐	T. Sales Prospect Cards, Sales Productivity, Conversion, Traffic Reports (Daily, Weekly & Monthly) and/or Customer Survey Forms						
☐	U. Sales Follow-Up Letters (with Coupons)						
☐	V. Grand Opening Invitations (and Others) with Placards						
☐	W. Community and/or Model Tour Guide						
☐	X. Children's Fun Book/Coloring Book						
☐	Y. Special Literature (Travel Club, etc.)						
☐	Z. Community Move-In Package						
☐	1) Publicity Reprints						
☐	2) Newsletter						
☐	3) Welcome Card						
☐	4) Change of Address Cards						

☐ 5) Booklet Containing Community and Area Information (Addresses, Telephone Numbers. Hours, etc. for Churches, Schools, Hospitals, Local Government Offices, etc.)

☐ 6) Builder/Customer Services Booklet (Telephone Numbers, Procedures, Guarantees)

☐ 7) Booklet Covering Residency, Insurance, Drivers License and Registration

☐ 8) Condominium/ Homeowners'Association/ Lease/Community Documents (Move-In Procedures, Fees, Pets, Complaints, Taxes, etc.)

☐ AA. Menus

☐ BB. Audio-Visuals. Films/ Recordings/Slide Presentations, Slide Viewers

12. SUPPLEMENTARY DESIGNS FOR MERCHANDISING, PROMOTION PREMIUMS AND OTHER GRAPHIC MATERIALS

☐ A. Ashtrays

☐ B. Athletic Fields

☐ C. Barbecues

☐ D. Benches

☐ E. Bicycle Paths

☐ F. Bicycle Racks

☐ G. Bike Pennants

Input / Preliminary / Presentation / Pre-production / Production Complete / Completion Delivery Install

NOTES:

		Input	Preliminary	Presentation	Pre-production	Production Complete	Completion/Delivery/Install
☐	H. Bird Houses						
☐	I. Blazer & Other Costume Patches & Emblems						
☐	J. Boat Dock						
☐	K. Bollards						
☐	L. Bridges						
☐	M. Bumper Stickers, Window Decals						
☐	N. Climbers						
☐	O. Clock Towers						
☐	P. Coasters, Napkins						
☐	Q. Crib Walls						
☐	R. Curbing						
☐	S. Decks						
☐	T. Edging						
☐	U. Fencing						
☐	V. Fishing Pier						
☐	W. Fountains						
☐	X. Gazebos/Shelters						
☐	Y. Place Settings: Glasses, Dishes, Silver, etc.						
☐	Z. Golf Cap & Gloves						

NOTES:

		Input	Preliminary	Presentation	Pre-production	Production Complete	Completion Delivery Install
☐	AA. Golf Carts						
☐	BB. Golf Course Markers, Flags, Score Pads						
☐	CC. Guard Rails / Railings						
☐	DD. Executive / Career Apparel						
☐	EE. Jogging Paths						
☐	FF. Kiosks						
☐	GG. Key Ring / Chain						
☐	HH. Ladders						
☐	II. License Plates						
☐	JJ. Light Standards						
☐	KK. Litter Containers						
☐	LL. Mail / Box Supports						
☐	MM. Matches						
☐	NN. Menus						
☐	OO. Mobiles						
☐	PP. Observation Points						
☐	QQ. Par-Course						
☐	RR. Parks, Birdwatcher or Nature Sanctuaries						
☐	SS. Pavilions						

NOTES:

		Input	Preliminary	Presentation	Pre-production	Production Complete	Completion/Delivery/Install
☐	TT. Paving Patterns/Blocks/Change of Road Texture						
☐	UU. Picnic Areas						
☐	VV. Placemats						
☐	WW. Planters						
☐	XX. Platforms						
☐	YY. Playgrounds						
☐	ZZ. Playing Cards						
☐	AAA. Recreation or Cultural Amenities						
☐	BBB. Resident Identification Cards/Decals						
☐	CCC. Retaining Walls						
☐	DDD. Sales Representative Badges						
☐	EEE. Sculptures						
☐	FFF. Shelters						
☐	GGG. Signage						
☐	HHH. Stadium Seating						
☐	III. Statuary						
☐	JJJ. Steps						
☐	KKK. Swizzle Sticks						
☐	LLL. T-Shirts						

NOTES:

		Input	Preliminary	Presentation	Pre-production	Production Complete	Completion/Delivery/Install
☐	MMM. Tables						
☐	NNN. Table Settings						
☐	OOO. Tennis Racquet Covers						
☐	PPP. Tents						
☐	QQQ. Tot Lots						
☐	RRR. Towers						
☐	SSS. Tree Guards						
☐	TTT. Trellises						
☐	UUU. Travel Club Badges						
☐	VVV. Vehicles (Tram Shuttle, Trucks, Buses, etc.)						
☐	WWW. Wheel Stops						
☐	XXX. Windbreaks						
☐	YYY. Wood for Play						
☐	ZZZ. Zoo Exhibits						

13. OFF-SITE SELLING

		Input	Preliminary	Presentation	Pre-production	Production Complete	Completion/Delivery/Install
☐	A. Welcome Center						
☐	B. Shopping Center Kiosk						
☐	C. Customer Sit-In						
☐	D. Broker Presentation						

NOTES:

	Input	Preliminary	Presentation	Pre-production	Production Complete	Completion, Delivery, Install
☐ E. O. & O. Office (Owned & Operated)						
☐ F. Fly-down Program / Package						

135

Appendix B
Project Development Checklist

PROJECT: _____

	Person Responsible	Due Date	Actual Date
Land Acquisition and Advance Planning Prepare market feasibility report			
Prepare constraints analysis			
Select consultants			
Prepare preliminary engineering study			
Prepare preliminary geology report			
Prepare preliminary site plan			
Prepare preliminary title report (a) Plot easements shown in title report			
(b) Clear any title defects			
(c) Distribute title report in-house			
Prepare preliminary project schedule, including critical dates list			
Prepare preliminary cost and profit			
Prepare preliminary cash flow			
Obtain Acquisition Committee feasibility approval			
Secure insurance for use of property			
Prepare tentative tract map			
Obtain ''will serve'' letters for sewer, water, and other utilities			
Planning Commission hearing (recommended approval of tentative tract map and Environmental Impact Review, if required, to City Council)			
Close escrow or execute ground lease			
Civil Engineering Select civil engineering firm and enter into contractual agreement			
Prepare final map(s)			
Prepare rough grading plans			
Obtain grading permits and pay plan check fees			

	Person Responsible	Due Date	Actual Date
Prepare improvement plan(s)			
Prepare budget			
Process improvement plans, pay plan check fees, and obtained signed plans			
Obtain bond amounts and post improvement bonds			
Prepare precise plot plan			
Prepare precise grading plan			
Obtain precise grading permits and pay plan check fees (if applicable)			
Prepare joint trench plans			
Obtain joint trench plan permits			
Prepare offsite bid packages			
Create documents showing areas of easements for maintenance			
Prepare condominium plan (if applicable)			
Prepare private street letter			
Prepare fill ground report			
Record final map			
Home Architecture Prepare preliminary plans			
Prepare preliminary plotting			
Prepare basic specifications			
Prepare final working drawings			
Prepare finish specifications (including color schedules and hardware)			
Prepare final plotting (including model complex)			
Obtain street addresses			
Prepare sales office construction drawings			
Prepare fence and arbor plans			
Obtain building permits			
Landscape Architecture Prepare preliminary plan and budget			
Prepare final working drawings			
Submit plans for plan check and pay fees (if required)			
Prepare use permit plan for sales complex			
Prepare recreation facilities plans			

	Person Responsible	Due Date	Actual Date
Project Development (Legal, Finance, Accounting, and Insurance) Hold submittal meeting			
Prepare C.C.&R's, articles of incorporation and by-laws (these may be required prior to recordation of final map)			
Prepare community association budget			
Select escrow company			
Submit documents to appropriate agency(s)			
Obtain final public subdivision report			
Prepare loan package (a) Acquisition and development			
(b) Construction			
Obtain approval of loan package by lender			
Record construction loan			
Bill applicable reimbursables			
Prepare option sheet			
Select flooring contractor			
Select community association management company			
Have management co. select maintenance vendors			
Attend community association organization meeting			
Attend community association first annual meeting			
Turn over community association facilities			
Prepare final cost and profit			
Escrow closing schedule			
Construction Offsite Obtain offsite bids			
Obtain utility contracts			
Award offsite contracts			
Pre-job conference			
Order construction signs			
Complete offsites			
Prepare map for sequence sheet			

	Person Responsible	Due Date	Actual Date
Construction Onsite Obtain bids on production homes			
Obtain bids on landscaping			
Place stamped construction plans in construction office			
Begin construction of models			
Complete construction of models			
Begin construction of production homes			
Final walk-through			
Marketing Select marketing consultants			
Advertising/Public Relations Agency/product orientation			
Project theme			
Mark/logo development and advertising concept			
Budget			
Media schedule			
Project brochure			
Ad development			
Merchandising Determine location of models			
Consultant orientation meeting			
Prepare offsite sign plan			
Prepare onsite sign plan			
Offsite sign installation			
Onsite sign installation			
Select interior designer			
Approve interior design plan			
Obtain carpet, flooring, painting, and special effects specifications			
Installation			
Model pick-up items			
Escrow Company Provide contract and instructions			

	Person Responsible	Due Date	Actual Date
Sales Staff office			
Manage interest list			
Prepare sales manual			
Fence plans			
Warranty book			
Equal housing opportunity logo			
Prepare lot files			
Stock sales office			
Prepare homeowners manuals			

ABC Advertising
Project Information Sheet

General   **Date** _____

Name of development _____

Address _____

Phone (sale office) _____

Name of developer _____

Address _____

Phone _____

Sales agency name _____

Address _____

Phone _____

Sales manager _____ Staff contact _____

Development hours _____

Name and phone number of contact person for further information _____

_____

Directions for reaching development from nearest highway or major street (include mileage if known)

_____

_____

_____

Project Summary for Public Relations and Advertising

Location _____

View(s) _____

Price range _____

Average lot size _____

Type of development (single-family detached, townhomes, etc.) _____

Architectural style(s) of homes _____

Innovative interior design and floor plan features _____

_____

_____

Especially desirable features _____

_____

_____

Recreational amenities _____

_____

Security features _____

_____

Energy features _____

_____

Area amenities _____

_____

Master Plan Design

Company _____

Address _____

_____

Phone _____

Landscape Architect

Company _____

Address _____

_____

Phone _____

Landscape Contractor

Company _____

Address _____

_____

Phone _____

Architectural Design

Company _____

Address _____

_____

Phone _____

Models Decorator

Company _____

Address _____

_____

Phone _____

General Contractor

Company _____

Address _____

_____

Phone _____

Type of development (single-family detached, townhomes, etc.) _____

Zero lot line? _____

Total site acreage _____

Current phase acreage _____

Total number of units planned _____

Units per acre, total site _____

Units per acre, current phase _____

Land ownership arrangement _____

_____

_____

If there is a homeowners association, what is the monthly fee?

_____

What does fee cover? _____

_____

Amount of land (if any) dedicated for use as permanent parkland or open space _____

Exterior Features

Type(s) of construction material

    Walls _____

    Roofs _____

    Exterior walls and siding _____

    Foundation (type and material) _____

    Driveway _____

Views? (describe) _____

_____

Separate sections of development designed for households with children?

(describe) _____

_____

Parking

    Private attached garages? _____

    Private detached garages? _____

    Carports? _____ Underground? _____

    Street parking permitted? _____

    Total guest spaces _____

    Guest spaces per unit _____

Setback from street? (describe) _____

Underground utilities? _____

Security Features

Will finished development be fenced? (describe) _____

_____

Guard gate at entrance? (describe) _____

_____

Visitor phone at entrance? _____

Electronic garage door openers standard _____ optional _____

Special door/window locks (types and location) _____

_____

Other special lock features _____

_____

Individual units fenced (describe) _____

_____

Burglar alarm or system (describe) _____

_____

Other security provisions _____

_____

Interior Features (indicate whether available in some, most, or all plans)

Type of heating _____ air conditioning _____

Fireplace(s)

  Which room(s) _____

  Wood burning _____ Other type _____

  Made of what materials _____

Private porches/decks/balconies _____

Connected with which rooms _____

Carpeting _____ In which room(s) _____

_____

Other type(s) of floor covering

  Kitchen _____

  Bathroom(s) _____

  Entries _____

  Separate laundry room _____ Location _____

  Prewired for television _____ Which room(s) _____

_____

  Prewired for telephone _____ Which room(s) _____

_____

  Prewired for cable _____ Which room(s) _____

_____

  Presale options available to early buyers (microwave oven, upgraded carpet, deluxe dishwasher, etc.) _____

_____

  Other special interior features _____

Kitchens

Dishwasher _____ Trash compactor _____ Garbage disposer _____

Oven _____ Gas or electric _____ Single or double _____ Self-cleaning _____

Cook top _____ Gas or electric _____ Microwave oven _____

Type of countertop _____

Type of cabinets _____

Type of sink (double, stainless, etc.) _____

Separate eating area (describe) _____

Pantry (describe) _____

Pass-through to dining area _____ to patio _____

Breakfast bar _____ Water line for ice maker _____

Other special design features _____
_____

Bathrooms

Double sinks _____ Marble or marble-like surfaces _____

Roman or sunken tubs _____ Atrium or plant area _____

Other special design fixtures and features _____
_____

Bedrooms

Walk-in closets _____ Mirrored doors _____

Fireplace _____ Other special design features _____
_____

Energy and Safety Features

Construction features _____

Insulation (type and R-value) _____

Gas and/or electric saving devices (describe) _____
_____

Water flow restrictors _____ Aerators _____

Solar-assisted water heating system _____

Water heater foundation _____ Solar panels _____

Smoke detectors (how many, where, type) _____
_____

Other energy and safety features _____
_____

Landscaping

Acreage to be landscaped _____

Percentage of site _____

Total cost of landscaping _____

Describe major transplants of full-grown trees, where applicable _____

_____

Is all landscaping provided, or will owners be responsible for some or all _____

_____

Other special landscaping features _____

_____

Recreational Facilities

Number of swimming pools _____ Size(s) _____

Number of hot tubs _____ Size(s) _____

Number of therapeutic pools _____ Size(s) _____

Number of tennis courts _____ night-lighted _____

Number of volleyball courts _____ shuffleboard courts _____

Clubhouse? _____ Which amenities will it include?

Sauna _____, card room _____, party room _____, billiard room _____, teen room _____,

gym/weight room _____, arts and crafts room _____, other _____

Surrounding Community

Major shopping centers nearby (existing and planned) _____

_____

Entertainment centers nearby (concert halls, movie theatres, restaurants, etc.)

_____

_____

Major business centers nearby (existing and planned) _____

_____

Parks, public golf courses, playgrounds, etc. nearby _____

_____

Major highways and/or streets serving the area _____

_____

Public transportation serving the area _____

_____

Schools (elementary, intermediate, high, colleges) _____

Day care centers in the area _____

Boy Scouts, Girl Scouts, other youth service groups _____

Are surrounding area property values competitive? _____

What is the projected increase in assessment value for the area? _____

Financial Information

Interim financing _____ Long-term financing _____

Source of home mortgage loan _____

Interest rate _____ A.P.R. _____

Total value of project _____

Total value of recreational facilities _____

Price range for units in this phase $ _____ to $ _____

Construction Schedule

Number of units in this phase _____ Tract number _____

(give dates below)

Groundbreaking _____ Sales to begin _____

Models open _____ Grand opening _____

First move-in _____ Completion of this phase _____

Completion of recreational facilities _____

Total project completion _____

Models and Sales Office

Names and/or plan numbers of decorated models _____

_____

Decorator(s)

    Company _____   _____

    Address _____   _____

    _____   _____

    Phone _____   _____

Carpets, drapes, etc. provided by   Sales office graphics by

    Company _____   Company _____

    Address _____   Address _____

    _____   _____

    Phone _____   Phone _____

Name, color scheme, theme, and target market of each model

Model 1 _____

Model 2 _____

Model 3 _____

Model 4 _____

Signage Programs

Does project have onsite signage? _____

Project identification sign? _____

Model identification sign? _____

Sales office sign? _____ Parking area sign? _____

Does project have offsite signage (describe and specify location) _____

_____

_____

Specifications

MODEL name/number						Comments
Low price						
Top price						
Square footage						
Cost/sq. ft.						
Average lot size						
No. bedrooms						
No. bathrooms						
Dining area-formal						
-open						
Other rooms-						
Garage-1 car						
-2 car						
-3 car						
-attached						
-detached						
How many of this model in this phase						

Glossary

Absorption   Rate at which a real estate project is sold or rented out, typically stated in units per week or per month.

Audit, competitive   See **Competitive audit.**

"Burma Shave" sign   A series of advertising signs designed to attract customers through the use of consecutive messages. Named after the shaving cream ads used for the Burma Shave product.

Capital Improvements Plan (CIP)   A proposed schedule of all future capital improvements to be carried out in a municipality during a specified time period, listed in order of priority with cost estimates and the anticipated means of financing each project.

Closing   An agreement between customer and salesperson to purchase a particular home.

Cluster development   A land development technique that groups structures and lots to provide usable open space and more cost-effective development. Density is usually based upon dwelling units per acre (d.u./ac.), with allowable units clustered on the most buildable areas of the site, leaving the rest undeveloped. Cost savings are achieved through reduced grading and shorter streets and utility lines. Clustering also provides cost savings to the local government through reductions in both maintenance costs and the number of recreational facilities needed. Distinction should be made between clustering of lots and clustering of units. Zoning regulations that permit lot sizes to be reduced from the usual standard to a predetermined minimum (from 10,000 sq. ft. to 5,000 sq. ft., for example), provide for the clustering of lots. Regulations that permit the use of attached and detached units combined, provide for clustering of units. Some **ordinances** permit the clustering of both lots and units simultaneously; others permit only the clustering of lots (see also **Density**).

Community association   An organization created for the purposes of owning, maintaining, and operating common facilities within a development to enhance and protect the owners' common interest. A community association is usually referred to as a homeowners' association in a **cluster development** or **planned unit development (PUD),** and as a condominium association in a **condominium** development. A condominium association differs from other community associations in that it does not actually hold title to common property or facilities; such property and facilities are held by individual condominium unit owners on a proportional, undivided basis.

Competitive audit   A written assessment of what types of product competing companies are selling and to whom, and how well the competing product is selling.

Comprehensive plan (master plan)   A document or series of documents that sets forth the goals and policies of a particular community or organization. Comprehensive plans are usually prepared by a community's planning department or by a consulting firm, and are reviewed and adopted by a planning commission and governing body. Comprehensive plans are based on considerable study and analysis of existing physical, economic, and social conditions in the community, as well as projections of future needs. The plan is considered comprehensive because it takes into account all current and projected aspects of the community, such as housing, transportation, schools, health care, and public utilities.

Conditional use   A use permitted in a particular **zoning district** only if the applicant can show that such use will comply with all the conditions and standards for that location as specified in a zoning ordinance and authorized by the planning board. Conditional uses are also referred to as special uses or special exceptions. In some states, the conditional use is granted by a board of adjustments; in others it is granted by the planning board.

Condominium   A form of ownership in which each unit, from inside wall to inside wall, is individually owned. In an apartment condominium, the structure, common areas, and facilities are owned by all owners on a proportional basis. In a **townhouse** and **single-family detached** condominium, each structure is the property of the individual owner, and the ground is owned and maintained in common.

Condominium association   See **Community association.**

Court   An open space, usually unobstructed from ground to sky, and enclosed wholly or in part by buildings or walls.

Cul-de-sac   A street having a single common ingress and egress with a means for turning around provided at the end. A variety of designs may be used. Most common are the square and circular configurations; hammerhead, Y- and T-shaped designs may also be used.

Demographics   Characteristics of the local population, such as total population and growth trends, household number and size, age, and income.

Demonstrate   To show a homebuying **prospect** the features that a particular unit has to offer; usually conducted by a salesperson.

Density   The number of families, persons, or houses per unit of land. Residential density is usually expressed as ''dwelling units per acre'' (d.u./ac.). Commercial and industrial uses are expressed as **''floor area ratio'' (FAR),** the amount of floor area permitted per acre of land. Gross density calculations are based on the total area of the site; net density calculations take into account exclusions for floodplain or other physical site characteristics. The term **intensity** is sometimes erroneously used as a synonym for density. **Intensity** has a broader meaning that refers to the level of activity on a parcel of land. It is commonly applied to commercial, industrial, and institutional uses.

Development   The construction, conversion, alteration, and any use or extension of the use of land. Also any mining, excavation, landfill, or land disturbance; and the construction, conversion, alteration, or enlargement of any structure.

Direct mail   Product literature that is designed for a specific **target market** and is mailed to that market for the purpose of advertising the product.

Duplex   Two single-family attached dwellings that share a common wall or floor in a side-by-side or back-to-back configuration.

Dwelling   A building or portion thereof used for human habitation.

Easement   A right given by the owner of land to another person, corporation, government, or entity for a specific limited use of that land.

Fair share   The number of units that can potentially be absorbed at a project, based on equal distribution of demand within a defined geographic area. Fair share is determined by dividing the number of projects expected in a geographic market area by the total demand projected for that same area (see also **Market capture**).

Fee simple   Commonly used to refer to individual ownership of a lot or parcel of land. Also, the most complete set of private property land rights.

Flag lot (pipestem lot)   A lot that does not front on or abut a publicly dedicated road, and where access to the public road is by private **rights-of-way** or strips of land.

Floating zone   A **zoning district** whose requirements are fully described in the text of the zoning ordinance, but which is unmapped. A floating zone designation is attached to a parcel of land in response to an applicant's petition for a **rezoning.** Once approved, the new zoning designation replaces the previous designation. This technique is commonly used for large-scale, comprehensive developments such as shopping centers, **planned unit developments (PUDs),** and industrial parks.

Floor area ratio (FAR)   The ratio of floor area to lot size permitted by the zoning ordinance. For example, a permitted FAR of 6.0 on a 10,000-square-foot lot would allow a building whose total floor area is 60,000 square feet. Commonly used to express **density** for commercial and industrial uses.

Focus group   A sampling of **prospects** who participate in an informal meeting for the purpose of determining customer preferences, needs, and motivations. Used as a **market research** tool.

Garden apartment (stacked flat)   A **multifamily** structure, usually 4 stories or less. Units are separated by a common hall, and share entrances, stairs, hallways, or other common elements. ''Stacked flat'' is a recent term for the garden apartment.

Homeowners' association   See **Community association.**

Infill development   The development of scattered, vacant sites in a built-up area.

Intensity   The degree to which land is used. While often used synonymously with **density,** intensity has a broader meaning and refers to levels of concentration and activity in such uses as residential, commercial, industrial, recreational, and parking (see also **Density**).

Market capture   The percentage of total demand from a specific market segment in a defined geographic area, which an individual development projects that it will capture (see also **Fair share**).

Market research   A scientific, statistical, and intuitive process used to learn about the customer market or group for a given product. Specific analytical methods are applied to data to yield required market information. Used as an aid in designing products for specific buyer markets based on customer preferences, needs, and motivations.

Master plan See **Comprehensive plan.**

Model A sample home that is used to show **prospects** the products being sold. Models may be decorated to appeal to specific **target markets.**

Multifamily A type of residential structure containing dwelling units for two or more households, where building entrances, stairways, halls, and other common elements are shared. **Garden apartments, stacked flats,** midrise and highrise buildings are common examples of multifamily structures.

Parapet The extension of a building's main structural walls above the roof level, commonly incorporated into firewall construction.

Patio home A single-family dwelling, usually on an individual **zero lot line** or conventional lot, that features an open **court** around which the house is built. The patio home is often, but not always, one-story, and is designed to bring together outdoor and indoor living spaces.

Performance standard A minimum requirement or maximum allowable limit on the effects or characteristics of a use, usually written in regulatory language. A building code, for example, might specify a performance standard for the fire resistance of a wall, rather than specifying actual construction materials.

Phasing (sales) A marketing and sales strategy in which a real estate project is developed and sold in increments. Sales phasing generally differs from production phasing.

Planned unit development (PUD) A form of **development** usually characterized by a unified site design that may incorporate a number of housing units and types, open space, and commercial and industrial uses. In its simplest form, a PUD may be several acres with a mix of housing types clustered to preserve open space. A more complex PUD may entail development of an entirely new town with conventional community elements, including commercial and industrial centers. PUDs offer many advantages, such as construction cost reductions for roads and utilities; greater marketability; and an enhanced sense of community through the coordinated use of open space, recreational facilities, and convenience to shopping and employment opportunities.

Pre-application conference Discussions held between developers and public officials, usually members of the municipal planning staff, before submission of a permit application or a **subdivision plat** approval.

Prequalify To determine that a potential customer is suited to your product, on the basis of preference, function, and financial status, before or during the customer's visit to the project (see also **Qualify**).

Pre-zoning A technique used by local governments to encourage development in selected areas of a community. Public facilities and appropriate **zoning** are provided to attract new residential, commercial, or industrial **development.**

Private street A road serving a limited number of lots, whose maintenance is the responsibility of the residents or the development company, rather than the municipality.

Promotion A special event designed to draw **prospects** to a project, generate good publicity, and increase sales.

Prospect A potential home buyer; a customer.

Qualify To determine that a **prospect** is suited to a product on the basis of preference, function, and financial status, prior to **demonstrating** the product. Enables sales personnel to direct prospects toward homes they can afford and that suit their lifestyle preferences (see also **Prequalify**).

Quadruplex (fourplex) A group of four attached units situated side-by-side, back-to-back, in a pinwheel around a common axis, or in a multiple-level configuration.

Rezoning An amendment or change to a **zoning** ordinance. Most commonly, rezonings involve changes in the zoning classification of specific lots or parcels. Rezonings can also be part of a more comprehensive revision to a local development master plan.

Right-of-way (ROW) A strip of land acquired by reservation, dedication, prescription, or condemnation for use as a road, crosswalk, railroad, electric transmission line, oil or gas pipeline, water line, sanitary storm sewer, or other similar use.

Rowhouse See **Townhouse.**

Setback Usually defined as the required distance between every structure and its front lot line. In some ordinances, setback refers to the required distance between a structure and all of its lot lines, also commonly called yard requirements.

Single-family attached Refers to a **dwelling** that is connected to other dwellings by means of common walls or floors (see also **Condominium, Duplex, Triplex, Quadruplex, Townhouse**).

Single-family detached Refers to an individual **dwelling** located on an independent lot (see also **Condominium, Patio home, Zero lot line**).

Site plan A plan showing uses and structures proposed for a lot or tract of land. It includes lot lines, streets, building sites and elevations and, in some cases, landscaping schedules and utility layouts. A site plan is more encompassing than a **subdivision plat,** which shows only lots.

Special exception   See **Conditional use.**

Special use   See **Conditional use.**

Stacked flat   See **Garden apartment.**

Subdivision   The division of a lot, tract, or parcel of land into two or more lots, tracts, or parcels or other division of land for sale, **development,** or lease.

Subdivision plat   A plan showing the location and boundaries of individual properties and streets within a parcel of land that has been divided into two or more lots, tracts, parcels, or other divisions of land for sale, **development,** or lease. A plat may simply be the device for offically recording ownership changes or lot divisions. In many communities, however, submission and approval of a subdivision plat is a prerequisite to building (see also **Site plan**).

Swale   A vegetated depression in the ground that collects and channels stormwater runoff.

Target market   The consumer audience for whom a product is designed and marketed, based on the results of **market research.**

Townhouse (rowhouse)   A single-family dwelling connected to other dwellings by common walls or floors in a side-by-side, back-to-back, or multiple-level configuration.

Triplex   Three dwelling units sharing common walls and floors in a side-by-side or multiple-level configuration.

Zero lot line (ZLL)   A **development** technique placing one or more walls of a building on a property line. This method is most commonly used by siting **single-family detached** dwellings along one side lot line. Smaller lots are more efficiently utilized by creating one usable side yard rather than two narrow ones. Covenants in ZLL developments generally govern the use and maintenance of lot line walls. ZLL configurations include staggered or "z" lots, angled lots, pinwheel clusters, square lots, and semi-attached units.

Zoning   The division of a county or municipality into districts and the establishment of regulations governing the use, placement, spacing, and size of land parcels and buildings.

Zoning district   A section of a county or municipality designated in the zoning ordinance text and usually shown on the zoning map, in which specific requirements for use of the land and buildings within the district are prescribed.

Bibliography

The Cluster Subdivision: A Cost-Effective Approach, American Planning Association, 1980

Community Applications of Density, Design and Cost, NAHB, 1983

Community Design Guidelines: Responding to a Changing Market, NAHB, 1984

Cost Effective Site Planning, NAHB, rev. ed. 1986

Financing Land Acquisition and Development, NAHB, 1987

How to Win at the Zoning Table, NAHB, 1985

Kitchens, NAHB, 1986

Land Buying Checklist, NAHB, 2nd ed. 1985

Land Development, NAHB, rev. ed. 1987

Planning for Housing, NAHB, 1980

Residential Development Handbook, Urban Land Institute, 1978

Zero Lot Line Development, American Planning Association, 1982

Zero Lot Line Housing, Urban Land Institute, 1981